Future Imperfect

Future Imperfect
Science Fact and Science Fiction

edited by
Rex Malik

Frances Pinter (Publishers) Ltd.,
London

Copyright © Sperry Univac, U.K. 1980

Published in Great Britain in 1980 by
Frances Pinter (Publishers) Ltd.
5 Dryden Street, London WC2E 9NW

British Library Cataloguing in Publication Data

Future imperfect.
   1. Literature and science — Congresses
   2. Science fiction — History and criticism
   — Congresses
   I. Malik, Rex
   501   PN55

   ISBN 0-903804-64-6

Typeset by Anne Joshua Associates, Oxford
Printed in Great Britain by A. Wheaton & Co. Ltd., Exeter

Cover design redrawn from a frame of film produced by Information
International Inc., Culver City, California.

The Parameters of the film were defined by their 'Digital Simulation
Processor' using a special 'Directors Language' developed by Information International Inc. with the frames recorded onto 35 mm film
directly using their Model FR 80 Colour Microfilm Recorder.

CONTENTS

FOREWORD

John Pascoe Marketing Director, Sperry Univac, U.K.

This book is the record of a seminar held at Sperry Univac's Executive Centre in St Paul de Vence, July 1979. This particular seminar is a regular event, an annual interaction between specialists in the field under discussion — whatever it may be — and senior technology journalists and broadcasters.

So what, you may well ask, is a large,.high technology corporation which operates world wide and specialises in the design, manufacture and sale of some of the world's most advanced computing systems doing sponsoring an enquiry into the relationship between science fiction and science reality.

The answer is a complex one, though there is a clue to be found in the description of our activity. We live and work in a technology which changes at a very rapid rate, a rate unique in the history of all technologies, and one which may to the outsider sometimes seem frightening. Between twenty and forty per cent a year improvement in performance for the same price — the industry refers to this as the price/performance ratio — is the historic norm since the industry began in the early fifties, and no end is in sight. Our own computers today are probably half the size and cost of their predecessors of as short a time as three years ago.

Had this rate of technological advance, of improvement in the price performance ratio, been matched by the aircraft industry over the last thirty years, you would by now be able to cross the Atlantic in seconds for less than the price of a packet of cigarettes.

At this point our interest in science fiction and its relation to reality might become a little clearer, for some aspects of the science fiction future are for us no more than our to-morrow, where for some other industries those same poss-ibilities are no more disturbing than a distant glimmer on the horizon.

It becomes obvious then that the consequences of our activities need thinking about, even if unconventionally so.

But that is the rationale behind a specific enquiry. The series of seminars are also linked by other considerations: we pick subjects which would normally 'fall through the cracks' in that while they are in everybody's interest, and thus everybody's responsibility, they are no one's specific responsibility.

There are in this instance no organisations set up to con-sider what role, if any, science fiction plays in society or its connection with reality. One cannot imagine a Royal Com-mission, or a legislative enquiry into the relationship, if any, between the two. Yet someone has to take the responsibility if such subjects are to be investigated and discussed in the way they deserve. So why not a company, one prepared to play the role of sponsor in the name of social responsibility? Sponsorship means what it states: we do not restrict the dis-cussion, neither do we necessarily approve, or disapprove, of all that is said at the seminars. The conclusions are those of the authors and those taking part. Our function is to provide the facility and let them get on with it. We do not try to push our own opinions: our experience has indicated that amongst an audience of this nature, it just would not work.

It is also important to realise that Sperry as a Corporation — and Sperry Univac — take the view that they like to listen to others and what they are thinking about the future. For in doing so it helps us to formulate our plans in order that we can ensure our survival in an ever changing world.

To ensure impartiality, we asked Rex Malik not only to help in the preparation of the programme, but also to chair the proceedings. As one of Europe's leading writers on computing and associated leading edge technologies and their effects we felt he was the right person for the task. After we had decided on the subject to be discussed, and in the course of preparation for the seminar, we were approached with regard to producing a book on the subject. We were of course delighted to give permission for this to take place and our agreement with the publishing company allows our share of the proceeds from the sale of this book to be given to charity.

As a result of this decision, Rex Malik was asked to produce this edited version of the event linked by his own commentary. We are grateful to him and to the participants who between them produced so much to think about. We hope that you will enjoy the results and be as stimulated by the ideas and opinions expressed here as were those of us who had the good fortune to take part.

PART ONE
Introduction

Rex Malik

The meeting had been called by the White House and was held in considerable secrecy. It brought together some of America's leading industrialists to consider the question 'What does the future hold?' It seemed after all that these were the men to ask; were not their companies, technology, and products changing the face of the landscape and the way we live, altering the present and making the future different from our expectations? They struggled with the problems to which the question gave rise for a couple of days without much success; until finally, in desperation, one of the participants commented: 'You should not really be asking us that question: you should be asking the science fiction writers.'

Which immediately in turn poses the question: is the comment worth taking seriously? Is there a reservoir of insight into the future to be found in science fiction which cannot be otherwise obtained by the use of more conventional techniques? Is science fiction seriously serious, and thus worth considering apart from its artistic insights into a future human, or other, condition? Have science fiction writers, knowingly or unknowingly laid their hands on the keys to the future?

Or are these questions portentuous rubbish? Is it possible that the breadth of science fiction is now so wide and the output so massive that some science fiction writers are bound to reflect some aspects of our future long before it happens? And that they do so in the same way that the old saw has it about the monkey placed at a typewriter: let him hammer away, and sooner or later, with luck without requiring immortality, he is almost bound to produce some of the works of Shakespeare. (This story too has already turned up in science fiction.) Put enough monkeys down and they will eventually reproduce what . . . the phone book?

This type of comment about science fiction is not just made by unfriendly critics. Science fiction writer Harry Harrison, perhaps best known for his book *Make Room, Make Room* (which became the film 'Soylent Green') the tale of a world in which population has outstripped resources, talks in these pages of 'science fiction shot gunning the future', the inference being that if you can fire enough shot in a broad enough pattern, some are almost certain to strike home.

Is the impact by volume all we can expect? Or is there a more serious, a more definable connection between science fiction and science reality, and thus our reality. And if there is that more definable connection, then is it quantifiable? If it is the latter, can we make more formal use of it directly, without requiring the intervention of interpreters, guides and go-betweens.

Again we are in danger of portentousness. Yet there is still a hard thought at the centre. Is there something here that we can get our hands on to our social profit, the easing of the human condition?

These were the thoughts I had when the notion of investigating the connection between science fact and science reality became a living project. They were the thoughts too that guided the selection of participants. And they were the only guide I had, for such an investigation had never been seriously mounted before. I expected that we should broadly follow these lines of enquiry. That we should investigate how good science fiction had been at predicting the future. It might well be that history repeats itself; the first time as tragedy, the second time as farce. But perhaps an investigation might indicate that it was the reverse.

I should have known better: chairmen may propose but, once on their feet, participants dispose. An enquiry is just that: the questions I was hoping to investigate turned out to be no more than a starting point.

It became clear very early on that another old saw had it: truth is stranger than fiction. This was so whether considering the history of predictions made by schools of past science fiction writers, or the products, many of which science fiction had only dimly foreseen: sometimes indeed had not foreseen, that had appeared.

But is this a general rule? One can say that it is so in the technology, the broad sweep of interests we call computing, which includes electronics, printing technology, magnetic storage, acoustics, telecommunications technology, power generation, library science, management science, and interests from a host of other disciplines particularly those clustered around mathematics.

Sitting in the room were some hundreds of man years of practical and observational expertise, some of the planets better computing reporters and television producers, as well as practising scientists, science fiction writers, skilled computer users, and computer company executives.

Naturally enough computing interests dominated the proceedings. And rightly so. It was not just that I had set out to put together a programme aimed at a particular sort of participant, a programme which would seek to contrast computer related science fact with its equivalent fiction. It was also that to me at least computing was the starting point. Beyond it lay machine intelligence, and that was to computing what the Space Shuttle is to the Wright Brothers aeroplane; sometimes indeed the contrast could almost be that of the Saturn 5, which powered the moon shots, and the balloons of the Montgolfier brothers.

And machine intelligence of course is a concept which lies at the core of any look at the future of computing. Yet it is also at the core of science fiction. Examine if you will almost any future world which does not postulate chaos, and some form of machine intelligence will be present. Machine intelligence indeed is an area where science fact and science fiction meet, they can do no other.

For machine intelligence in more than embryonic form one has to remember is still in the future. Yet its issue predates both computing and science fiction as we have come to understand them. The concept of machine intelligence is central to two of the recurring major myths of the race, myths which many science fiction writers have also played upon: one is the legend of Rumpelstiltskin and his never ending cornucopia, the other that even more potent legend of Frankenstein.

There are undertones of both legends, and others, in many of the papers. And they do not always arise where you expect them to. Thus Professor Frank George's paper on science reality manages to combine, it would not be unfair to write, Frankenstein, and muted though they may be, echoes of 1984.

If I foresaw that this was going to happen, that we should end up dealing knowingly or not with myths that are common, myths with a long history, I was not prepared for something else. I wrote some paragraphs that back the obvious: that fact is stranger than fiction. Now I knew that the question, what is the relationship of science reality to science fiction, was going to cause problems. It is after all a naive question — which was one of the reasons it was asked. However, I did not realise that it was going to cause so many problems. For in turn, it begged a question: what is science fiction?

The just as naive reader will assume that science fiction is a product of the twentieth century, and can probably name a handful of science fiction writers most of whom will be alive today. But that is only part of it. Though the name science fiction is of twentieth-century origin, science fiction as a distinct genre is a much older literary form. Professor I. F. Clarke, a literary historian, evidences recognisable science fiction — as distinct from future mythology which is older — from as far back as 1644: indeed he has even written a book in which that date is in the title. (*The Pattern of Expectation: 1644-2001.*)

We think too of science fiction as something sparked off by technological or social developments to which has been applied a literary imagination, something therefore with pretensions to being a literary art form, even if only a minor one. Certainly it is at least this. It has its own rules and conventions which mark it off from other forms of fiction. And even if those are more occasionally than not broken, that too is in the western literary artistic tradition.

However, above all, to get science fiction into print, it has to first give an assurance to its originators and backers that it will make somebody money. It has been an offshoot of commercial publishing, whatever may have been the initial spark that caused a particular work to be written. The point is neatly made by I. F. Clarke when he discusses Northcliffe's publication of the 'Invasion of 1910' in the *Daily Mail.*

The result is that much masquerades as science fiction which does not justify the name, if one is to take a purist 'can it help in our current preoccupations' line. Science

fiction is a term which covers a wide range of writing, much
of which cannot be dignified by calling it literature. In it is
found future history, fantasy, cops and robbers, surrealism
and even 'lo the poor Indian': pop sociology in fictional
form. What is science fiction engages and enrages — among
others — I. F. Clarke, Harry Harrison, A. E. Van Vogt, and
Heinz Wolff. Read for instance Harry Harrison's intemperate
comments on page 73. But if a successful practitioner of the
craft cannot be intemperate about the field in which he
makes his living, who can?

And this is not the only problem that trying to arrive at
some clear cut definitions can raise. If science fiction does
relate to science reality or fact in any meaningful way, in
what way does it so relate? That point is much discussed in
science fiction circles. As both Ray Bradbury and Arthur C.
Clarke have pointed out, and A.C.C. repeats it here, in
his interview, there is a school of science fiction writers
who discuss the future not so much to predict it as to prevent it. And just to confuse matters, not all science fiction
writers who would take this view necessarily take it all the
time.

Some science fiction attempts to be predictive, and from
the same writers at that. For instance, Arthur C. Clarke tries
to do just this in *The Fountains of Paradise*, the tale of a
future attempt to connect earth satellites and earth directly
by the creation of a 'space elevator'.

And then, to confuse matters further, there is the science
fiction writer as philosopher. A. E. Van Vogt, though he
would not call it that, instances one example of this on page
85. Science fiction writer Robert Heinlein attempted it in
Starship Trooopers, and got called a fascist for his pains.
Isaac Asimov grapples with philosophy in the *Foundation*
series, as he grapples with almost everything else. And
Arthur C. Clarke again did so in what many, myself included,

regard as his best book, *Childhood's End.*

I could go on. But it becomes apparent that the label Science Fiction is a convenient method of subsuming a lot of disparate fiction which would otherwise prove unclassifiable. Except that: the notion of change is common to all forms of science fiction, it is the root that all works share.

But science fiction does not have that all to itself. It shares a concern with change with a wide range of other speculative literature, writings which have roots not in the imagination of one or more authors, but in science fact, and its exterpolation. One can call it the literature of forecasting, for that is what it tries to do as coldly and as clinically as possible. The techniques used are many and varied, but they all share one thing in common: they try to present a view of some particular aspect of the future on which people can base action, can plan, and that on a rational basis.

Much of the enquiry was concerned with just this sort of literature. And it soon became apparent that something unusual and unexpected was happening. Science fiction was being generally far outstripped by this school of science fact. It might not be that truth is stranger than fiction, though it generally is: it was that conscious rationality is far outstripping imagination.

It is not only that one was outstripping the other, it is also that there is a confusion of form. The boundary between hard science fiction and predictive science fact is a fuzzy, unclear one. And it leads to a problem in its turn: how do you distinguish between the two?

It may be that the methodology to achieve the results will differ, but how can you tell when what you hear could be mistaken for either. On which side of the boundary, for there has to be such a boundary however fuzzy it may be, lies what?

For instance, might not an example of science prediction

look also like an example of hard centered science fiction to the point that the two seem interchangeable and hard to distinguish. Does it matter if the two get confused? Well yes it does; their purposes are different and their uses are different. It may well be that science prediction is used by science fiction as a springboard; it is not usual for the situation to work the other way around — though one or two minor examples are given in these pages.

The confusion of form can have interesting consequences: there are two examples of this given. One is to be found in Earl Joseph's discussion of the future of micro electronics, in which for instance he discusses how micro electronic farming could be made to work. The other is in a paper by this writer which describes how the low temperature operational requirement for Josephson junctions might be satisfied.

Both papers come out of a long involvement with the technology: either could be read as science fiction — or science fact, it depends on the audience and its interests and qualifications.

Was the enquiry then worth holding? That is for the reader to judge. It is not the last word that needs to be said on the subject: indeed it is almost the first. Neither does it come to conclusions; rather it describes, compares and investigates.

But I for one came away with my preconceptions about the relationship of the two substantially modified: I knew more. And one of the things I now know more about was the differences in the process of producing either science fact, which really should be called science speculation, and science fiction.

The two are different (even though they can be confused). Yet they were not always so, as the first investigation shows. Once upon a time, and that was not so long ago, there was only speculative writing. The exterpolative literature of science speculation did not exist, and neither did the classifiable science fiction, though fantasy — the myth — had seemingly always been with us.

So here is I. F. Clarke with a fragment of the long, rich, and complex history of speculative writing.

1 THE FUTURE AS HISTORY

I. F. Clarke

Professor I. F. Clarke is Chairman of the Department of English Studies at the University of Strathclyde, Scotland. His bibliography of futuristic fiction The Tale of the Future *is now in its third edition. His other books in the area are* Voice Prophesying War, *and* The Pattern of Expectation.

Futuristic fiction is the mode evolved naturally by a technological civilisation to consider itself.

During the last two hundred years the description of the future — for entertainment in innumerable science fiction stories, and deadly serious in the classic utopias and dystopias — has grown into the most popular and often most effective form of fiction.

Futuristic fiction cannot, and does not, seek to predict the future in the manner of the futurologists. It seeks, and at times is able, to prophesy events, social changes, great technological developments that later come to pass. The success rate is minimal. Perhaps one story in thousands comes anywhere near to discerning the shape of things to come.

Reasons for this lie in the highly specialized nature of futuristic fiction and, especially, in the profound relationship between a society and the kind of prophetic fiction that writers generate. Futuristic fiction is essentially an image-building activity and at its most compelling a highly moral operation. It has been developed and perfected during the

last two hundred years as the one form that can most perfectly respond to the possibilities, hopes and fears, delights
and dangers of a technological society.

My first proposition then is that though the term Science
Fiction has been widely used, I would argue that it is only
one part of the vast and very varied field of futuristic fiction.
The 'Tale of the Future', the 'Zukunfts Roman', 'Le Roman
de l'Avenir' are European terms for a form of fiction that has
evolved over the last 200 years, a series of stereotypes:
specialised forms of various kinds which have emerged from
time to time in order to deal adequately with certain aspects
of a technological civilisation in the course of continuous
development. Two of the earliest of these forms have been
the 'Ideal State of the Future', the great prophetic form —
especially of the nineteenth century — which in its various
ways did so much to crystallize and project the admired
capacities of the Victorian epoch. The first of them, now
long forgotten, was a best-seller in its day, Sebastien Dermier's
L'an de 2440. It begins in the year 1771, and starts one area
of speculation about the future and about the form of
society. About the same time the first of the grand old
disaster stories appeared, introducing the *On the Beach*
syndrome. The *Doctor Strangelove* syndrome, which begins
in 1805 with the European success, a best seller, *Le Dernier
Homme* (*The Last Man*), this was translated into most European languages and gave Mary Shelley the idea for a book of
the same name, *The Last Man*: Byron also wrote poems
about it.

The notion we have of ourselves and our capacities in a
technological civilisation has caused the evolution of a whole
series of specialised forms that range from the constructive,
ideal state (*The Last Man*) onto the wars of the future (the
Zukunftskreig, Les Guerres Imaginaires), which were a minor
publishing industry in Europe between 1870 and 1914.

There are also the great admonitory myths, the class Distopias of modern times, Yevgeny Zamyatin's *We*, Carol Kapec's *R.U.R.*, George Orwell's *1984*, Aldous Huxley's *Brave New World*, and Kurt Vonnegut's *Player Piano*. And there is the vast boiling malestrom of science fiction, the most popular fiction form, I would argue, today. What Verne called, not science fiction but 'Les Voyages Extraordinaire' and what Wells, the founding father of modern science fiction, knew as 'the scientific romance'.

So to the second point. The tale of the future is the natural literary product of a technological civilisation: without technology there is no futuristic fiction. In consequence, the tale of the future has always been symbiotic with, and often parasitic upon, the Press. From the beginnings in the late eighteenth century, the writers have found their material in the specialised journals. Today the latest reports about artificial insemination, cloning, spare parts surgery, proposals for space colonies, and the rest of it, very rapidly find their way into speculations and stories. A classic example is Wells. Wells gave the word, or the term, 'Atomic Bomb' to the English language in 1913, when he described, in *The World Set Free*, for the first time a war fought with atomic weapons. Wells got those ideas from the reports he had read on the work of Rutherford and Soddy who were the pioneers on the investigation of the atom, and in particular, he got a great deal of his information, cribbing almost word for word, from an article by Frederick Soddy, 'The Energy of Uranium', which appeared in *Harper's Magazine* in 1908. Going back to the beginnings you find Cousin de Granville's story of the last man of 1805, which he began writing in 1798. His ideas came from two of the most important pamphlets of that year, and in fact of that century. One was Jenner's 'Enquiry into the Causes and Effects of the Varioli Vaccini', which gave vaccination to the world, and the other, in the same year, a couple of months later, was the classic statement about population contained in Malthus's 'The Essay on the Principles of Population'.

Cousin de Granville took these two ideas and came up with a remarkable statement about the future. His deduction was that with Jenner giving life, and Malthus promising the end of humanity if we were not careful, the population would explode. In 1805 the citizens of Europe could read Cousin de Granville saying 'God has limited the time of humanity because an additional motive for this limitation is the profound improvement He is making in medical science by which thousands of the infantile world have been snatched from the empire of death, and who, in thus becoming the heads of numerous progenies, are laying the foundation of an immense population which the world in after ages will be inadequate to sustain.'

The third point I would make is that the tale of the future does not and cannot predict the future in the sense that the technological forecasters strive, as accurately as they can, to achieve a prediction of the future. It seems to me that futuristic fiction is essentially an image building activity and that, whatever form it takes, its main operation is to project upon the blank screen of the future selected contemporary hopes, fears, and possibilities. Indeed this is more or less the point that Bernard Wolff makes in a postscript to *Limbo 90*, published in 1952. He says that he is writing about the overtone and undertone of Now in the guise of 1990, because it would take decades for a year like 1950 to be milked of its implications. The year 1950 was, of course, the year in which the first successful computer UNIVAC went to work and started up the anxieties and the horror stories about the computers. *Limbo 90*, and the sequence of stories that followed, revives an ancient myth, 'The Sorcerer's Apprentice', in which human beings do not make proper use of the gifts of the gods.

My final point is that in order to appreciate the immense range of futuristic vision, I suggest that it is necessary to see the future as a unique literary mode, a major development in European technological civilisation in the first instance, and nowadays of course throughout the world. It had its origins in Europe, rapidly becoming transatlantic, and it is now largely a world form. A hundred years ago the Japanese had not produced a single futuristic story, although the Emperor was a passionate reader of Jules Verne. He read everything published and Jules Verne was translated into numerous Japanese editions. It has only been in the last 40 or 50 years that the Japanese have developed their own science fiction stories and, of course, they are now turning them out in vast numbers. The genesis of it can, I think, quite properly be likened to the idea of progress, out of Darwinism, with technology acting the part of midwife. In 1841 Tennyson, in the thudding verse of *Locksley Hall*, sums up a poet's essential idea of the future. He too speaks with the optimism of that time, describing himself thus:

> I, the heir of all the ages,
> In the foremost files of Time.

That evolutionary notion of humanity was spreading in the last century. Developing this new idea of 'the future' he writes

> I looked into the future,
> Far as human eye could see
> Saw the vision of the world
> And all the wonder that would be.
> Saw the heavens fill with commerce
> Argosies of magic sails
> Pilots of the purple twilight
> Dropping down with costly bales.

Essentially this expresses the Victorian idea of the future at a moment in a poet's life, at a moment in the history of a continent when the future seemed to be absolutely unalloyed and progress certain. The genesis of futuristic fiction can be seen in its evolution: taking its time, its information, its cue from the great social and industrial changes of the last 200 years.

In the beginnings you get the first intimations of futurity from James Watt. In the 1760s and 1770s, Watt was at work on the separate condenser, the steam engine, the great workhorse of the first Industrial Revolution. The proof that mankind was beginning to move into a new kind of future, that man would control nature and that the old ages of wind and muscle power could end and would end came for all Europe in the extraordinary and spectacular demonstrations of the first balloons. In 1783 the first hot-air balloon went up. In November 1783 came the first manned flight when human beings ascended first over Paris and later over the principal cities of Europe. The inhabitants could look up and see what for most Europeans was an extraordinary and marvellous development. The sky, which had been for millenia the home of the gods, the home of the saints, the place to which one ascended after death, this area had suddenly been conquered and if proof was wanted that mankind could control nature, it was up there. Then Didero, a tough and hard-bitten old philosopher, founding father of the Encycle Verdi, fell on his knees, they say, and cried out that one day men would go to the moon. That experience was really the turning point, and from the 1780s onwards the European consciousness of its increasing power over nature begins to inform the view of the future. For the first time in the history of humanity, images of the future were being produced by the engravers. You get the first image reproduced throughout Europe, the first hot-air balloon going up from Versailles with its load of a cock, a sheep and a pig. Why those three, I don't know. But that extraordinary event began to generate a series of images. These are the first, futuristic images ever developed: the engravers look into the future and they see the possibility of balloon travel and thinking in the stereotype of that time they can only think of ships, so they hang underneath the balloon a vast ship — a total impossibility. They immediately begin in the imagination to apply this to war. And in 1798 they illustrate the idea of what balloon warfare could be like with trumpets, muskets and people potting at each other.

In a German print of 1801, the old and the new combine in the notion of vast aerial armadas all bombarding the troops who are set up in the classic nineteenth-century style. The possibility of balloon travel, transatlantic travel, of which Mary Shelley wrote in *The Last Man* (1825) is here. The hopelessly, untechnological ideas of the draughtsmen are in there and yet, prophetically they are expressing their belief in the capacity of someone, some time to create a vast air machine which will get people across the Atlantic.

Even more elaborately, in the early 1800s, when Napoleon was planning the invasion of the British Isles, the Napoleonic propagandist engravers made an impact. They built a tunnel secretly underneath the Channel for the invading army. Hydrogen balloons were brought from France and the heroic fighter forces of the British Isles are ascended, suspended from kites and, apparently armed with ten-foot long scissors, attempting to cut the balloons of the other side.

At the same time the engravers, contemplating Napoleon's plans for invading the British Isles, looked into the future and asked why not 'landing craft'? They produced an accurate representation of a floating machine invented by the French for invading England, which acted on the principles of both wind and water mills, carrying 60,000 men and 600 cannon, practically an entire French army. The technological

elements are imaginatively feasible, but the image belongs to
the world of the future. These engravings were circulated by
the hundreds throughout Europe, and they could be seen in
the coffee houses and in shop windows. There were other
variants with a vast citadel in the middle and water mills
working like made.

There is another type: they produced a representation of
a raft and an apparatus, as invented by the French for the
proposed invasion of England. Again the notion was that the
French, if they got the right wind, and everything worked,
would stagger ashore one day and complete the subjugation
of the British Isles.

Here for the first time in history are the consequences
of the new imagination generated by technology. From the
early 1800s to this day, that process of thinking about the
future in many ways has continued unchanged. Writers and
graphic designers have been drawing from comparable
sources, space colonies, spare part surgery, cyber-men and
such like. It is from this vision that they have developed the
image of the future.

I said earlier that the tale of the future has grown, changed
and evolved in close collaboration with the Press. One of the
more remarkable examples of this is Jules Verne, the founding father of science fiction, who was made by and also made
his fortune out of, the Press and, by collaborating with his
publisher, like all good authors are supposed to do, not only
did he make an even bigger fortune for his publisher, a matter
of dispute between them later on, but also gave the world,
no longer just Europe, those classic images of the future
which summed up the great Victorian notions of the human
potential. The golden story of Verne's life begins round
about 1861 or 1862 when, unknown to Verne, the publisher
(probably the most successful publisher in France in his day),
P. J. Hetzel, was pondering the increase in the population,

which was going up like a rocket, and the ever-rising level of literacy. In the 1860s, it occurred to him that there would be an opening for a new type of magazine, aimed at adolescents, dealing in part with science but science presented in a special way. By pure chance, Verne entered his room with his first manuscript. Hetzel read it and this crystallised his thinking. In 1867 the collaboration began when Hetzel founded the famous influential magazine, *Le Magasin de Information et de Recreation*, which ran until the early 1900s and was the most popular journal of its kind in France.

Verne wrote his stories for the magazine but the remarkable fact is that although Verne wrote for adolescents, in many cases it was the adults who took him up, read him, popularised him and serialised him in their papers. The eminently respectable *Journal des Debains* took the serial rights of *From the Earth to the Moon* and published that account day by day, and in the process trebled their sales. There are other similar successes for the publishers. What had happened was that Verne's formula for removing a great deal of reality from his stories worked. He found a new set of rules for writing for the young; no passion, and no argument about politics, unless it was about the rotten British who were colonialists (he always biffed them as much as he could). But apart from this simplification, his heroic narrative was admirable for many adult readers. And so Verne, in presenting these epic stereotypes of human possibility attracted the attention of adults everywhere and today is read widely throughout the globe. In *20,000 Leagues Under the Sea* Captain Nemo's vast submarine (the like of which we have not yet seen, not even in the nuclear submarines) is driven by electricity. We find Rover, forever circling the world in the Clipper of the Clouds, or Barbignan and company who are blasted to the moon in the Columbia. Note well, the command capsule of Apollo 11 was called the

Columbia in memory of and in homage to Jules Verne, who, in providing the image of lunar travel from the earth to the moon, had set many people thinking about new directions.

Well, Verne wrote the world's first, universally successful science fictions. Were they true forecasts? Not in any engineering sense could it be said that they predicted or described the future. But, I don't think that matters. They were true prophetically because they provided a society with magnificent successful and potent images of its most admired and realisable (or apparently realisable), ambitions. The great power of Verne and of this kind of writing is to be seen in its effects. Simon Lake, one of the successful pioneers of the submarine, drew the inspiration for his own career from Verne. Again, Santos Dumont, another pioneer of dirigible flight, has written in his biography that the first notions that he ever had of what he would like to become resulted from reading Jules Verne. There is of course the great-grandfather of space flight, Constantine Tsiolkovsky. He said he got his first notions about rocket dynamics and the possibilities of inter-planetary travel from that great fantastic author, Jules Verne. 'He directed my thoughts along certain channels and then came an idea and after that the work of the mind.' And from Verne to Tsiolkovsky, to Hermann Oberth to Werner Von Braun, there is a chain of ideas, possibilities, images that direct and command the attention of writers and of the entire society, so that intellectually there is this new language, these new idioms that say 'space travel', 'the conquest of space' and so on.

What Verne did for science fiction a now long-forgotten, but in his day notorious, English writer did for another unique form, the tale of future warfare. The writer was Colonel Chesney, finally Sir George Tompkins Chesney. He was a colonel of engineers, one of the first of the new kind of educated soldiers. In January 1871 he wrote to

William Blackwood of *Blackwood's Magazine*, one of the
great and successful editors of the last century, suggesting
that he should write for *Blackwood's* a short story about an
imaginary German invasion of the British Isles with a total
conquest of the British people. His objective was to put over
the message that in the new circumstances of 1871 there was
but one answer for the British people and that was conscription. The story he produced was undoubtedly the most
successful and widely read pamphlet, in English, in the last
century. It was 'The Battle of Dorking' and it appeared in the
May issue of *Blackwood's*, 1871, and the explosion that followed was worldwide. It derived its power and its ideas from
a number of contemporary facts. The first great fact was that
in the war of 1870 the Germans had beaten the French and
ominously had displayed new kinds of warfare. Innovations
included breech-loading artillery and above all the rapid concentration of troops by the railways, which had never been
seen before. One used to calculate on three weeks to get
troops from reserve positions to somewhere near the enemy,
but the Germans were doing so in days by the railway. That
was one ominous image of the future. The other was of
course the condition and state of the British who on seeing
the change in the balance of power became extremely
alarmed.

Chesney set out to write a didactic story which would say
'look now, and think about conscription'. His story is remarkably well written, holding together well and told in a
series of brilliant episodes. The Germans land: a magnificent
military operation. And the battle is largely left to the volun-
teers, the equivalent of the Territorial Army, who are, of
course, heroic but completely overrun, and the British people
are defeated. Then follows, although he is writing for his
grandchildren, the account of what it is like to pay taxes,
how horrible it is. The sensation shook the nation for about

three months. The Prime Minister, Gladstone, was forced to get up in public and tell the nation not to listen to such alarmist stories, as the Germans had no intention of invading. There were translations into most European languages, French, German, Italian, Spanish, Swedish, Dutch, with two editions in Canada, and three in the United States all of which were pirated. In Australia there was an edition and also in New Zealand — and it went on like that. In addition there were literally dozens of stories about the other side of the Battle of Dorking which said that the Germans did land but we beat them in the end.

Here is another unique form of fiction emerging, which is marvellously adapted to the needs of belligerent nation states, all equipped and equipping themselves year by year with a military technology which they think, innocently, will allow them to fight the old style of Napoleonic wars, with battles over in a day and everything finished by Christmas. What Chesney did was to generate this specialised form which was taken up throughout Europe, setting the style and the pattern. The Germans began to write these things, followed by the French and hardly a year went by between 1871 and 1914 without some of these appearing and some years they appeared by the dozen. The classic example is the even more notorious case of *The Invasion of 1910*, which was written by William Le Queux, Queen Alexandra's favourite novelist. Northcliffe, of the *Daily Mail*, had the wonderful idea that in 1906, with the Germans arming, and the beginnings of the *entente* with the French, it would be good for sales if he could get somebody to write about a German invasion of the British Isles. He approached William Le Queux, and Northcliffe being Northcliffe, also sent for the Commander in Chief of the Imperial General Staff. Lord Roberts came, humbly knocking on his door and the brief was this, to write with William Le Queux the military side of the German invasion. So Roberts rapidly produced a successful and sensible military plan with major forces running North East and South of London and a very rapid German advance. When Northcliffe saw this he was much incensed, being a Press baron, complaining that the Germans must go into every town and village where the *Daily Mail* was read. Exit Lord Roberts and enter Le Queux sketching an absolutely lunatic but magnificently successful invasion of 1910. 'Wigan Pier captured by the Germans'; dragoons galloping through the streets of little towns in the Potteries; people rowing ashore in boats from every port from Leith down to Southampton. When they went to press in the *Daily Mail*, Northcliffe organised hundreds of sandwich men, all dressed in Germany military uniform, to walk with placards saying 'The Germans are coming'. Of course the effect on the sale of the *Daily Mail* was most gratifying, and the book sold over 2 million copies. I have discovered so far 22 foreign translations, including, God help us, Chinese and Arabic. What the Arabs made of it in those days I do not know.

Let me present one more example of a slightly more serious side of this — this happy, continuing cooperation between experts and Press, from the illustrated magazine, *Black and White*. This came out in the early 1890s, and one of the first things the editor did was to commission from eminent military and naval authorities a fictional account of the Great War of 1892. (They loved these stories about great wars.) What this editor did was to get hold of Admiral Colomb, one of the most eminent sailors of the day, Colonel Morris who was a major figure at the Staff College and remarkably good writer on tactics, and a variety of other people including *The Times* correspondent from Berlin. These people, all experts in their way, collaborated in describing the Great War of 1892. Here is the editor chatting up the readers.

The air is full of rumours of war. The European nations stand fully armed and prepared for instant mobilisation. Authorities are agreed that a great war must break out in the immediate future and that this war will be fought under novel and surprising conditions. All facts seem to indicate that the coming conflict will be the bloodiest in history and must involve the most momentous consequences to the whole World. At any time the incident may occur which will precipitate the disaster.

The editor of *Black and White* considering that a forecast of the probable cause of such a struggle will be of the highest interest . . . etc. . . . .

What emerges from these writers who quite seriously and accurately applied their contemporary specialist knowledge to *The Great War of 1892* is first, a fairly accurate political forecast. There is an attempted assassination in the Balkans and this causes the Serbs to mobilise, the Austrians to mobilise and, in effect the fatal chain of events of 1914 are prophetically seen here. Then the Great War breaks out. The battles of that war last, on the whole, three or four hours. The troops advance in close column, they are met with rifle fire and at sea the normal tactic is ramming, with limited fleet engagements. But there is one moment when the authors come close to foreseeing what actually happened. They describe an attack by the Russians, a night attack, upon German entrenched positions, with the Germans using searchlights; as the Russians come up, 10,000 of them, they come against barbed wire and are mown down. In describing this, they comment on the importance of barbed wire, and yet, remarkably, fail to generalise. They are thinking so much in the stereotypes of their time of a war of movement that they do not foresee the possibility of a great line of entrenchments with quick firing artillery, machine guns and the rest of it all there. If they had thought of that then they might have been even more prophetic.

In Wells' famous short story, *The Land Ironclads*, he describes armoured fighting vehicles which are used successfully against entrenched troops. But he was just writing a short story; he fails to generalise and does not see the potential in the massed attacks of the tanks.

The most remarkable forecast actually comes from Conan Doyle. In June 1914, in the *Strand Magazine*, he published a short story, *Danger*. In this he describes a successful war fought by submarines in which all shipping approaching the British Isles is sunk. This was shown in manuscript to eminent admirals of the day and all of them said 'this is absolutely impossible'. In fact one man who later became the Commander in Chief, South Western Approaches said, 'It is inconceivable that any naval officer would ever sink an unarmed merchant vessel.' Within six months the Germans were doing it every day and of course were posing a major threat.

Conan Doyle was right and he was wrong. He was writing in a biased way not because he was trying to prove that submarine warfare would come this way. Rather, he was arguing for a tunnel underneath the Channel — he was one of the great propagandists for it — and he was trying to produce a series of arguments in fiction which would convince everybody that the one salvation for the British people in 1914 was to have a Channel tunnel. So, the images, the projections and so on are in their way often very deceptive.

PART TWO
Introduction

Science fiction and science speculation are both essentially democratic activities: (Even a moment's reflection will show that they have to be so. Both must assume that the people in some number have to be present: both must recognise that as ever, we the people will continue to be awkward, difficult, subject to the whims of change, and to changes of whim, and liable to impose differences from the postulated future on the most carefully elaborated and researched of constructs. In other words people are . . . people.) Yet, when you leave the world of politics and the short term future, the world of the same as before but a little better, the people are seldom asked for their opinions. Whether or not they should be, nuclear power or supersonic aviation are not normally subjects for democratic decision, however much some groups of society wish they were. Society may apply science and technology, but in many major areas it does so without first obtaining a democratic consensus.

So what do the people want: and what do they expect? Let us wheel on stage the first ever limited, but still nationally representative, opinion poll mounted within a democratic society — and thus by extension in any society — which sets out to test a few common ideas about the future, and about belief in some of the ideas often found both in science fiction and in science future fact.

The poll was conducted by John Barter, the experienced Managing Director of National Opinion Polls Limited. He used the occasion not simply to pose pre-set questions and ask for a yes or no but also to ask people what sort of inventions they would like to see, and more than 800 people made suggestions. Many of those suggestions are in fact the subject of both science fact and science fiction, some indeed such as the matter transporter could have come straight out of 'Star Trek'.

Yet there is already a sense in which one can consider that speculative literature, whether of the factual or fictional kinds, is already a democratic activity. Now I realise that this notion may at first sight, and given the above, seem strange; yet it is not when you consider where the bulk of such work, and such literature, is produced. The contribution of the socialist countries to the literature is minimal. Another moment's reflection will show why this should be so. Any construct of the future which would be acceptable to the people has to deny some 'essential' part of the present. It has to state, even if by inference, that some condition in the present is unacceptable. That if we do this, or let this happen, the future will be either better or worse.

But how are those in the socialist countries going to deny that the present is unacceptable: how can they do more than state that it is a necessary step on the road to socialism, and that the blueprint for what socialism is to be is already laid down? Both are crippling to the imagination. Even worse, both restrict the intellect and cut off from the writers an examination of alternative futures, certainly those which would allow for possibly different political ordering of society scenarios.

The democratic nature of science speculation is nowhere more clearly spelt out than in the two pieces which follow, pieces full of sharp disagreement. Frank George is unashamedly a future believer, one who thinks that the future should be different from the past and who believes that the contribution made to that future by the technologies which are also bringing it about is massive and to be supported, even if he must sound warnings about some of the possible uses the artefacts and techniques can be put to. It would not be unfair to call Professor Frank George's view of the future conventional: this is the way a cultured, humane, highly intelligent expert practitioner in the field of change thinks and feels, and there are many more like him even if they do not articulate the views quite as clearly.

By contrast Heinz Wolff will have none of it. He believes as he tries to demonstrate that in many areas the real change that has so far happened has been minimal. The title of his piece, 'The future is further off than you think', was jocularly imposed on him one night over dinner. What he has made from it is a *tour de force* which I find persuasive even if my instincts say to me 'I think he is wrong'. But then Heinz Wolff can be very persuasive. I had to introduce him with the phrase that Andre Gide once used about Andre Malraux, only the name has been changed. 'In the presence of Heinz Wolff, one does not feel like an intellectual.'

There is no way in which the George and Wolff views of the future can be reconciled. The only point on which one can take comfort is that as neither set out to be predictive, both are likely to be wrong. Which will be more wrong is of course open to argument, and which a reader will approve of has perhaps more to do with the reader's predilections than the likely future.

2 ATTITUDES TOWARDS SCIENCE FICTION

John Barter

> *John Barter, a Chartered Accountant educated at the London School of Economics has been involved with market research since 1962. He is Managing Director of NOP Market Research Ltd., and currently (1979-1980) Chairman of the Market Research Society.*

We thought it would be interesting to find out a little about what people in Britain believe is likely to happen in the future and their reactions to various possible material, political or social changes.

NOP Market Research Limited therefore carried out a survey of 2027 adults aged 15 years and over using a systematic probability sample designed to be representative of all adults in Great Britain. Interviewing on the survey took place between 5th and 10th July 1979.

First we asked people about their belief in the possibility of intelligent life away from this planet.

Q. Do you think there are intelligent beings in the universe, apart from on earth?

	Sex			Age		
	All %	Men %	Women %	15–34 %	35–54 %	55+ %
Yes	44	48	41	55	48	29
No	37	37	37	30	34	47
Don't Know	19	15	22	15	18	24

	Occupation		
	White collar %	Skilled manual %	Unskilled manual %
Yes	49	46	37
No	34	36	42
Don't Know	17	18	22

More people believe that there is life elsewhere in the universe than reject the proposition. Men, young people and white collar workers are most likely to accept it.

When asked about the specific phenomenon of flying saucers, there is rather more doubt, but even so it seems remarkable that two people in every five believe there is some truth in the reports of flying saucers.

Q. Do you think there is any truth whatsoever in the reports of flying saucers visiting earth?

	Sex			Age			Occupation		
	All %	Men %	Women %	15–34 %	35–54 %	55+ %	White collar %	Skilled manual %	Unskilled manual %
Yes	40	39	40	54	39	25	42	42	34
No	46	47	45	33	47	59	44	43	51
Don't Know	14	14	15	13	14	16	14	14	15

Men, white collar workers and the over 55s are more sceptical about flying saucers but more than half of the younger people accept that there is some truth behind the stories.

The next question related to science fiction directly, and asked:

Q. How much of what science fiction writers write about do you think will come true? Out of every ten things they predict, how many do you think will happen?

On average people believe that about three out of every ten predictions will be fulfilled. The largest groups are the 28 per cent who do not believe any of the things will happen and 19 per cent who believe half the predictions will come true. The differences between men and women and between the different age and occupation groups are not very great except that the older people are the most sceptical with 41 per cent of over 55s believing that none of the things science fiction writers write about will ever come true.

We next explored reaction to a number of possible developments by asking our sample if they believed they would happen in the next fifty years or if they would ever happen.

Q. Which of these things do you think will happen?

	Happen in next 50 years %	Ever happen %
One world government	9	30
Control of weather throughout the world	18	38
People will settle in other parts of the universe	23	60
No more shortages of food and housing	9	25
Considerably worse shortages of food and housing	64	—
A single world language	8	29
A world wide war destroying millions of people and buildings	24	68

People are rather pessimistic about the future with two-thirds foreseeing considerably worse shortages of food and housing in the next fifty years, a quarter expecting a destructive world war within fifty years and 58 per cent predicting such a war at some time. There is no 'ever happen' figure for shortages of food and housing because some people think there will be shortages in the short term but that these will eventually be solved. It is interesting that people see human problems are more intractable than technical ones. Twice as many of our sample think that we will eventually settle in other parts of our universe as think we will achieve one world government or a world language. Similarly it is rather horrifying that so many foresee a major world wide conflict.

It was surprising to find that men and women were almost at one in their predictions for the next fifty years with only control of the weather being thought substantially more likely by men than women.

In the long term men were much more likely to feel that we would achieve a single world government (though they were not asked whether they thought this would be good or bad). Nor were there substantial differences in age, though the 25–34s were the most pessimistic both about shortages and about the possibility of a world war in the next fifty years. Over a greater period young people think one world government, control of weather and settling in other parts of the universe are probable to a greater extent than older people, but it is still the 25–34s who fear the worst.

Occupation groups also have a fair measure of agreement about what will happen, though the white collar workers are more inclined to feel that some developments will take more than 50 years.

In the following section of the questionnaire the emphasis was changed from what people expected to what people would like to see happen.

Q. Which of these would you personally like to see come about?

(a) Fully safe computer controlled cars.
(b) Self-cleaning, self-adjusting clothes which don't wear out.

(c) Light bulbs which last for ever.
(d) Completely safe and reliable methods of contraception.
(e) Machines to do all the household tasks, operated by the voice.

Results are given in the table on page 36.

Here, we asked people whether or not they would like to see certain things happen but did not ask why. For this reason any commentary on the reason for the results can only be conjectured. It may be that only just over half our sample wanted fully safe computer-controlled cars, because the others felt it would take the fun out of travelling or because they feared that such a development would have undesirable secondary effects of some sort. It is surprising to see on this, as on most of the other answers, so little difference between men and women, and it is difficult even to venture a guess as to why the Scots should be substantially more in favour of this development than any other group.

Self-cleaning, self-adjusting clothes that don't wear out are the least popular of the suggestions put forward and it may be that this is because people feel that it would be very boring to have such clothes which would kill fashion and stifle individuality. There were very few differences between the various groups on this matter, though white collar workers were least in favour.

Is this further evidence that men are now as fashion conscious as women?

We can only be baffled by the fact that anyone other than a light bulb manufacturer does not want light bulbs that last for ever, and yet 16 per cent of our sample did not support the proposition. Perhaps this is a reflection of the fact that however beneficial a new development is, some people will oppose it through suspicion or obstinacy.

It is to be expected that not everyone will support the idea

Those who would like to see:	Sex			Age			Occupation			Region				
	All %	Men %	Women %	15-34 %	35-54 %	55+ %	White collar %	Skilled manual %	Unskilled manual %	Scot-land %	North %	Mid-lands %	Wales West %	South East %
(a)	56	58	55	58	62	49	58	57	53	71	56	50	55	56
(b)	39	39	38	40	38	39	32	40	46	39	39	37	43	39
(c)	84	84	83	85	85	82	86	83	81	86	84	87	85	81
(d)	77	77	78	86	85	62	83	77	70	72	77	77	78	79
(e)	41	47	36	44	42	37	40	41	42	42	42	36	38	43

of completely safe contraception and the figure of 77 per cent in favour seems quite high. However, the opposition (8 per cent) is actually lower than for any of the other four things (even everlasting light bulbs!), and the 15 per cent 'don't knows' on this question are the highest. Support for safe contraception from the 55+ and unskilled workers is balanced by highest 'don't knows' in these groups.

Voice operated machines to do all the household tasks were the one development revealing fairly sharp differences between men and women. They found favour with 47 per cent of men, but with only 36 per cent of women. Although women would chiefly benefit by this change, perhaps they feel it would threaten their position in the home.

Having made people think about quite a number of suggested developments in the survey, they were next asked what other inventions they would like to see come about. It is known that people are generally not very good at producing their own ideas in answer to questions like this but nevertheless it was rather surprising that two thirds of our sample — seven out of ten women — could think of *nothing* that they would like to see come about.

The two most popular suggestions concerned advances in medicine and alternative sources of energy. 9 per cent of those interviewed mentioned developments in the medical field or cures for diseases with 4 per cent making specific mention of cancer. 11 per cent talked about alternative or cheaper sources of energy with 5 per cent specifically mentioning a substitute for petrol. Solar energy, a matter transporter, and the use of the sea each attract 1 per cent.

Various forms of labour saving devices in the home or the garden were suggested by 4 per cent of the sample while 3 per cent mentioned new or safer methods of transport and 2 per cent pollution control.

By and large those interviewed were not very inventive and

although men and white collar workers made rather more suggestions than the other groups, the sorts of things they suggested were not markedly different.

Many people believe that in the near future a substantial proportion of workers will be able to, or be required to work from home, and we decided to explore reactions to this idea.

Q. Present developments mean that it may soon be possible for many people to work from home rather than going to an office or factory. Would you welcome this yourself?

	Sex			Age			Occupation		
	All %	Men %	Women %	15–34 %	35–54 %	55+ %	White collar %	Skilled manual %	Unskilled manual %
Yes	35	32	37	38	35	31	32	37	36
No	59	63	56	58	62	59	63	57	57
Don't Know	6	5	7	4	3	11	5	6	8

Only just over a third of all adults would welcome this development. This might be because people fear the actual change in their work which would be necessary, or because they would not want to lose the aspect of communality from their job which gives them a chance to get away from the home environment.

Women are rather more in favour than men possibly either because they see more opportunities for combining running a home with interesting work, or because it might enable them to see more of their menfolk.

We also asked a supplementary question:

Q. Do you think this would make people generally more contented?

	Sex			Age			Occupation		
	All %	Men %	Women %	15–34 %	35–54 %	55+ %	White collar %	Skilled manual %	Unskilled manual %
Yes	27	25	28	32	25	23	21	29	30
No	65	68	61	61	68	66	71	63	59
Don't Know	9	7	10	7	7	11	8	7	11

People were even less convinced that working at home would be good for others than they were that it would be good for themselves.

Before presenting the results of the survey, the same questions were asked of the seminar delegates and contributors. Compared with the general public they were:

More likely to believe in intelligent
    beings in the universe.   67 per cent against 44 per cent
Less likely to believe in flying saucers   18 per cent against 40 per cent

3   SCIENCE FACT — WHERE IT LEADS

Frank George

*Professor Frank George is Head of the Department of Cybernetics
at Brunel University and Chairman of the Bureau of Information
Science. His books include* The Brain as a Computer; Computers,
Science and Society, *and* Man the Machine.

I don't really regard science fact and science fiction as
being particularly different. Science fiction does speculate
about things which could happen, whereas science fact tries
to make them happen more often than not. And the reasons
they don't always happen are economic or sometimes, there
is a strong social feeling against certain developments. I think
for instance the reason that programmed instruction and
teaching machines did not get off the ground was largely a
matter of social pressure and vested interest on the part of
teachers. There was certainly a feeling that there was something wrong about having machines teach people. There are
these biases against machines generally which have to be overcome, if indeed it is agreed that machines can play an important part in society.

The obvious analogy is with ordinary fiction and its relation to factual writing. I often have the impression that
novelists — I am thinking of people like Iris Murdoch,
Anthony Powell, C. P. Snow, rather British biased — talk
more about reality than people who write biographies and
historical studies. Certainly the difference is marginal. I think

the same difference applies here, therefore I don't think of
science fact (and we called the book I edited about two
years ago *Science Fact* to distinguish it from science fiction)
as being essentially different. I think they are really dealing
in the same coinage.

One of the points I would like to make right from the
beginning is that I think there are grounds for pessimism and
reasons for doubt about the future for a variety of reasons,
which I will try to explain. One of them undoubtedly is the
exponential rate of growth. Knowledge is growing at an enormous speed, especially in the fields of science and technology
where such a rate of growth has never before been known.
Let me give one simple example. About twenty years ago,
the Canadians decided to do a lot of hydro-dynamic equa-
tions, necessary to allow ships to come from the Atlantic into
the Great Lakes, to Chicago and places like that. It was
reckoned that it would take every available mathematician in
Canada (and Canada is not completely bereft of mathematicians) some hundred years to do all the computational work.
The University of Toronto's computer did it in about two
weeks. A computer today could do it within a matter of
seconds. That rate of growth is fairly astronomical. Another
fact (admittedly an estimate — rather like the kind of
estimate that says the brain contains 10^{10} cells, or, after some
thought, 10^{11}, not a big difference just astronomical) leaving
aside the philosophical implications because they have not
changed that much, the amount of knowledge we have
learned and the amount of factual information we have
learned in the last twenty-five to thirty years is more than we
have learned in the whole previous history of humanity. If
this is regarded as any indication of the rate of exponential
growth, then the next ten, fifteen, twenty years will show a
startling change in civilisation. And we ought to be prepared
for it. We ought to be prepared for the worst, even if the best

happens. In cricketing terms, I always like a long stop when I'm keeping wicket, so if I am wrong and things go better than they seemed to be, so much the better. But my fear is not so much in technological change *per se* as the philosophical and sociological implications. I'm not a prophet of gloom but I feel that one should be warned against the dangers of the possibilities. What is known as the Mini-Max Regret principle expresses this rather eloquently.

'The computer is a moron' is not I think a sensible statement to make because a computer *per se* is just like a human being without the brain put into it. And many people with their brain put in are morons — let alone without them. You cannot talk about computers without considering the program and the programming method used to develop computers in their techniques. And the reason computers are used is because they are the only universal economic machine in which we can actually simulate various features of human behaviour. But will forecasting change anything? One has to distinguish firmly between two kinds of forecasting. In our present knowledge of meteorology, forecasting rain tomorrow does not change whether it will rain tomorrow or not. But if I forecast unemployment in for instance Yugoslavia tomorrow then I might well be able to change it because people listening to the forecast will realise that they must take certain steps to change things in the light of the forecast. So a failure to distinguish between forecasts which do have an effect and those that do not would be a great mistake. I would like to think that the things we say here will have some effect, however slight (I quite admit they may be slight) on the world around us.

There is a well known inability for the expert often not to see the wood for the trees. A friend of mine, following a talk I gave in Bristol many years ago about the possibility of replacing organs, like hearts, wrote me a nice little note (he was Professor of Chemistry there at the time) saying, 'George, you really do say some ridiculous things'. Well, George admitted that he did sometimes say some ridiculous things. But he was not ridiculous on this score, because transplantations took place within five years. Another example is the case of the Astronomer Royal, who said that going to the moon was nonsense, about five or six years before it actually happened. The reason why experts are so bad at seeing the implications in their own field is because they only see one little bit of the whole particular jigsaw puzzle, they're concentrating on *the* sea, or *the* ship or *the* sky, and they don't usually see the whole picture.

Seeing the implications of what one does is one of the biggest difficulties of all. The vitally important part of seeing the implications is undoubtedly what we call the imagination. It is not possible for a human being to make sensible decisions without being able to envisage the outcome of the decisions they take. And this is being imaginative. If I do X, what will happen if I do Y, what will happen if I do Z? Of course there are a lot of techniques, decision-making techniques, linear programming and the like, and off-the-cuff techniques which have to be often combined or bent to suit the particular situation. But in every case, you have to try and see what the likely outcome is. Often we go back to the Mini-Max Regret principle and say to ourselves, well we'll do the thing that is likely to cause us the least pain if we're wrong. It's rather like being asked to bet on a horse race. If you're asked to bet twenty pounds of your money, it doesn't too much matter what you do. You perhaps look for a couple of winners. If you are asked to bet two thousand pounds, you're a bit more careful and spread your bets. If you are asked to bet twenty thousand pounds, you are very careful and your attitude has actually changed from thinking you might win a bit of money and if you don't it doesn't matter, to being rather more careful, to thinking to yourself, 'my God all I've got to do is to avoid losing too much!' These are the sort of considerations that one has to bear in mind.

The scientist — and this is I suppose what science fact is all about — is always concerned with combining information 'off-the-shelf'. This is why it is necessary to have a reference library memory. If we are going to simulate human intelligence, it's a reference library mentality we want. We are not so concerned with what we know, in terms of how to do things, we are much more concerned with how to find out what we do from somebody else. We want to know who to go to and say, 'look Charlie, you're the expert on queuing theory, tell me what I do with this particular type of problem.' In fact, if I was asked to build an artificially intelligent system in the next few years, my concentration would be entirely on the reference library approach because this is absolutely vital. It's knowing how to find information that really is important. Because we, the human species, store most of our information in the environment.

Coming to my own particular field, this is really what we are concerned with. We are concerned with artificial intelligence and we're concerned with simulating or synthesising (there is a slight difference: simulating means actually trying to do it the same way as human beings do it, synthesising is achieving the same ends or better ends by any methods at all) which means looking at; sensing, how do we take in information from the environment; perception, how do we interpret that information; learning, how do we adapt to changing circumstances; thinking; how do we not only learn but symbolise events in our environment and then manipulate the symbolisation of those events — which leads us straight into logic and language. And if there is one huge step which takes human beings above the other animal species, it is the development of the use of symbols and particularly the development of the use of languages. Now, all these things are becoming a reality. They're complicated but they're growing at an enormous rate. Computer languages, dealing with natural language programming, languages which allow people to talk to computers in English, synthesise English and recognise English speech, are all things which have happened in the last five to ten years. They are realities and I sometimes get the impression, listening to people who talk about science fiction, perhaps critics of science fiction, that they do not realise the rate at which our knowledge is progressing. An awful lot of these things can be done now. Admittedly, if I was asked to say what is the biggest flak, it is the fact that the work is piecemeal. You can synthesise or simulate perception, you can do the same for learning, for thinking up to a point, and decision taking (which is really part of thinking) you can do it for language or logic, but it is very difficult to put the whole thing together because the size of the operation is so considerable. What is difficult, and it is the one human ability which on the whole we have not yet discovered how to realise in computer terms (in computer terms means simply, artificially), is the ability to extemporise.

It is the flexibility which is so difficult to achieve. This is part of the imaginative process. On the other hand you must not, of course, run away with the idea that if you wanted to build a chess playing machine for example, you are not the smallest bit interested in just writing a program that plays chess. Any fool can do that. What you are interested in doing is an interactive program which teaches the computer how to learn to play chess, which is a very different thing. You have to inculcate into the computer, by means of a certain type of programming (which is known as heuristic programming) the technique of accumulating information and utilising that information by making its own inductive and deductive inferences. And it's a little bit more than that too. Talking about inductive and deductive inferences suggests classical logic, but I do mean much more than that. I mean practical reasoning. Any way in which you can formulate generalisations, and utilise those generalisations to practical ends (and this is perhaps the point which distinguishes practical reasoning from classical logic, this is why if you pick up a book on classical logic you are slightly misled about the nature of thinking) is that practical reasoning is goal-orientated. You are usually asking yourself 'I have a goal or a set of goals, how do I achieve that set of goals, what sort of means do I use'. Logical, Probabilistic, Statistical, etc. etc. However classical logic does not tell you anything about the goals you might be able to achieve, it only tells you what is logically inferrable from the starting point that you have. Whatever axioms you set down, it tells you what permissively follows it. And that has, of course, nothing whatever to do with your goal orientated behaviour, as it stands, which has to be given the goal to give it its purposive aspect. And this is very much a part of what we have to do if we are going to try and achieve human intelligence artificially.

Now, I suppose one of the questions is, how far along the line are we? This is quite difficult to decide. We spend a lot of our time in the department arguing about how much we have achieved, how much we have not achieved. It is like the old joke about a pint of beer, half drunk: are you concentrating on how well you have done, or how much you still have to go? The more we learn in a way, the more we realise we need to learn. And certainly if you look at it from a simulation point of view, translate it into the human brain, and ask how much we know about the cerebral cortex and the role the reticular formation plays and even the hypothalamus (which is I suppose a relatively simple part of the human brain) and the central nervous system generally, one is delighted by how much one knows, and yet, horrified by how much one does not know about the particularities. But, of course, this only applies to the simulation problem, it does not apply at all to the synthetic problem, where we are working on computer programs, which often simulate what are neural nets or logical nets not necessarily representative of the human brain at all. It does not matter if they do not do it the same way as long as they do it.

So, one has greatly mixed feelings, but one of the biggest issues that has cropped up in the last year in our own discussions among people who have an interest in artificial intelligence is the extent to which consciousness, awareness, self-awareness, etc., is a vital part of the process of intelligent behaviour, and whether it can be reproduced artificially. I think the answer is that you cannot get a system to make intelligent decisions of the kind that humans generally make without having self-awareness. It is also closely bound up with language because as soon as you start using language and start talking about 'I believe so-and-so', or 'My impression is . . .', you obviously must have self-awareness, otherwise the words you are using make no sense at all. So, the self-consciousness aspect of it, the imaginative aspect of it, seems to follow inevitably from the construction of the system. This leads me on to a side issue. In the relation between structure and function, to what extent does the functioning of the system depend on the structure? My own feeling is that it may in some ways but not in others. I am not sure, cannot be sure, how important it is, any more than I can be sure how long it will take to produce an artificial intelligence system, equal in ability to human beings.

One thing is clear though, that if we do achieve an artificial intelligence system equivalent in ability to human beings (and I personally do not doubt it, though I am not at all sure it is a good idea) it is quite obvious we can improve on them.

Once you have the idea, you do not have to be restricted by the actual size of the cranium, size of the body and other biological constraints which would not occur in an artificial intelligence system. It would not be necessary for example to have a brain and limbs all connected in the same place. There is no reason why the brain should not be in Alaska and the limbs in Arkansas and Bournemouth or anywhere else. There is no reason why they should be connected directly. This direct connection, the autonomy of the human being is a biological 'accident'. So the question is this: how soon will this step take place? The step is to get up to the level of human intelligence. The answer is, I do not know, but forgetting that, I suggest within the next twenty or thirty years. And if it does that, it will be surpassed it in forty, fifty or sixty years, perhaps less.

What are the social implications of this? I think it is going to change the nature of society considerably. This is the feature of our own development and research which interests me most. So much so that when I have occasionally talked on television or radio in Britain, America and Australia I often get someone saying, 'Do you think you are doing something which is actually going to impair the nature of society'? I hesitate, have a quick scotch and say, 'I think that if I did not do it someone else would.' Human curiosity is not a basic feature of human development, people will do it.

Much as I would like to see humans being retained to to jobs, I can not see it remaining possible when the factor of ability between the machines doing the jobs and the human beings becomes so great that it is hopelessly uneconomic to use human beings at all. So human beings are going to be paid just to exist. We are going to develop and inhabit a very much more complicated welfare state than we have already.

The fact remains that it is not difficult to destroy the structure of society by making it more complicated. It is much more difficult to organise, to make decisions, to do things intelligently today, precisely because you know more. And this is self evidently true. If you only know three things it's no problem, you can only do one of three things. But if you know thirty-three things it is a great deal more difficult, you have got a much wider choice to make. And what science — science rather than technology — has done is precisely to provide a situation where we have many more complicated decisions to make. This in the short term has consequences. One is that society is in some respects more chaotic, and in some respects more ordered. It is the more ordered that worries me most. It is the bureaucracy, and the trend towards totalitarianism which I fear most from the 'databank society' which we are setting up. I suppose nothing illustrates it better than the position of the police. One says: I wish to goodness they were more efficient. And then they become more efficient. If you are stopped on the road, within a matter of seconds in some countries (and it will soon be true in Britain) they can find out much of your life history. If all the databank information is put together, the threat to the community is enormous: there is no privacy. The threat to human privacy is one of the biggest single dangers in the modern development of science and technology.

The possibility of a machine species follows obviously from what I have said. We might well manufacture a machine species which, if it becomes more intelligent than us, might well decide to take us over. I do not think they would bother, but it depends what you mean by the phrase 'take us over'. Just to eliminate would seem to be the simplest way. It depends whether they had the same cheerful attitude towards us that we have towards our Great Danes. And on the whole, when I think of our Great Danes and I think of us, I think it is very unlikely that they will have such a charitable attitude. The fear of the machine take-over, i.e. take-over by an

artificially constructed species constructed by our own ingenuity has a certain humorous ring, a touch of Monty
Python about it. But, more seriously, I think that what is
going on in scientific departments is an important issue.
There are a number of departments in America, Europe,
and Britain, all under different names. Sometimes called Departments of Information or Departments of Communication,
they often surpass science fiction writers in the sort of
speculative ideas they put forward. The reality, which I say
with some hesitation because I do not know quite enough
about science fiction to say it unequivocally is that I do not
know whether they have looked at the social implications
sufficiently carefully. Certainly the social implications I
take to be very dangerous indeed and the only reason for not
stopping it is that one person stopping it would not stop the
rest of the world doing it.

It seems much more sensible to keep on warning people
about what is happening in our society. We are becoming an
artificial society, the sort of society which is represented
by the kind of food they serve on airplanes. A sort of plastic
society, in which we are losing sight of some of the more
important values in life. This of course raises the question,
what are the more important values in life? I do not want to
make the mistake that Aldous Huxley made in *Brave New
World*, that of standing outside the situation and saying this
is what is happening, they are being conditioned. That was
the early behaviourist influence, of course, which he was
drawing attention to. He, himself, often relapsing into Shakespeare and saying, 'Isn't it all ghastly.' Failing to recognise
that he was being conditioned, or would have been conditioned, by the same society as all the rest. You cannot stop
the world and get off. So we have got to be careful that we
do not get involved in such a way that we cease to be able to
stand aside and ask ourselves what sort of world we want.

What sort of world do we want? I do not know the answer to that. But, there are two things that do stand out in my mind which are clearly relevant to the present world. Obviously the decay of religious belief is a major factor, and this has come about almost entirely because of philosophy and science. There is no doubt about that. Logical positivism and scientific knowledge generally have made the stories of Christianity and other religions to lack credibility, and if they lack credibility they do not have the influence, the social influence, the cement influence they originally possessed. We all lose by this. Is there any way in which we can reconstruct the stories? My hope is that we can, I do not know, if anybody is imaginative enough in science fiction to do some religious fiction, but it must be credible if they do it. It is through the imaginative and the artistic which come very near to religion in many ways that we might find a way out. I suspect we shall go back not to an international society but to a tribal society, a small tribal society living in a far simpler way, without the desire to have fourteen television sets, or however many the average is.

Therefore, a tribal society, which at the same time is probably organised in a hierarchical fashion (through Europe and America, eventually under some sort of international control) might be the way of getting the best of both worlds. However it is the two problems put together, the threat of modern science and technological totalitarianism which are the main causes of worry. A Government which has a great deal of scientific knowledge, which means a great deal of control over the community will exercise that control. One can see us in Britain easily slipping into a totalitarian type of state, but no doubt this could easily also happen in France, Germany, America. That is one of the worries.

How do we deal with it? I think we try and deal with it through the use of the imagination in a more artistic direction. I cannot believe religion qua religion will ever quite make the grade again. It's a bit like — for those of you who know football in England — Huddersfield Town. I cannot somehow believe that they will ever get back into the First Division.

What sort of society do you want? What kind of life do you want? Now, I know what kind of life I want. I want to live it in the countryside of Buckinghamshire and I do not mind if I never leave it: in the country, with the trees and the peace, with the Great Danes, of course, and away from it all. But this may merely be because I am in my dotage, and it may be that younger people feel quite differently. Anyway, whatever you want it is certainly important that you ask for what you want. And I would like to place the emphasis more on philosophy and thinking in philosophical terms, than I would on science and scientific terms. Science is a process which is self-generating, which is going to go on regardless. I would like to see us ask philosophical questions about the nature of science and its implications for society. I do not mean the philosophy of science: that is quite different, I mean philosophy and the implications for our social future. That is what concerns me as a practising scientist more than any other single thing.

Finally, I should pay tribute to science fiction. It has the great merit of making us think about things which we might not otherwise think about. That science fiction works are of enormous help is undoubted, but do the writers think enough? I know there are some like Ray Bradbury who spring to mind who do, but do they all think enough about the social implications of what is going to happen or what is likely to happen, and whether we want it to happen. It is the impact of what is happening more than what is happening which is my main concern.

4 THE FUTURE IS FURTHER OFF THAN YOU THINK

Heinz Wolff

Heinz S. Wolff is Head of the Bio Engineering Division, Clinical Research Centre of the Medical Research Council, and is best known to the public as the adjudicator on such television programmes as 'The Great Egg Race'. He is the author of Biomedical Engineering *and has published over 70 papers.*

I work in bio-engineering, a field very close to medicine, an emotive field in which the application of technology touches almost everybody, so I recognise myself as being in perhaps a peculiarly sensitive situation.

I have not read much science fiction, and what I have read I did not like, so you will excuse me if I make some rather jaundiced remarks about what I believe are its three forms.

The first form is I think essentially a way of disguising a thin story line with technological glitter. Both the reader and the writer find it less demanding to be impressed by some scientific development than to have to identify with the motivations and the emotions of real people. It is not fundamentally different from an old style Western, which was undemanding because the rules were clearly stated; the white hats were the goodies and the black hats were the baddies, and no deep understanding was required. There is of course a sub-set, such as Batman, a very elementary form of science fiction, where merely endowing the characters with the capacity to do certain things which are known by the reader to be impossible, makes it easier to write the plot.

The second, and in my view slightly more respectable, form of science fiction is what I call literary expressionism. I have stolen this word from the painters, who find it useful to transform their perception and their message by clothing it in a form which is disconnected from the action which it portrays. It is easier to communicate a message if you take it out of the real world and put it into a world where the rules, customs and facilities are slightly different, and this seems to me to be a perfectly legitimate way of expression.

The third type is the 'Real Message', or the prophecy, where people intend really to look into the future and to portray it with (as Arthur Clarke says later) the possibility perhaps of preventing some event or of alerting the population or the government to a particular contingency. This I suppose is really the most respectable type, and I fear by far the least common.

I would now like to explore what I meant by the catch-phrase 'the future is further off than you think'. It is my view that the impact of technology in depth, as distinct from its impact as a sort of veneer — like having a pocket calculator in your pocket — is a much slower process than the fore-casters, particularly the Jeremiahs, imagine.

I want to take you on a journey in time. Imagine that, when you fly to England from France, quite imperceptibly as you are approaching London your aeroplane changes to a de Havilland four-engined aeroplane, the type of plane which flew a service between Lyon and Croydon in 1933. So that by the time you land at Croydon it will actually *be* 1933. And I would like you to ask yourself, assuming that you belong to the same income group as now (an important quali-fication), how long a re-familiarisation period you would really require before you were relatively comfortable. You would take a taxi, only a bit more angular than expected, and you would be driven to your home. And ask yourselves, what would actually have been so very different? I think you would find that once you had taken away the television set, and replaced the domestic machinery by somebody who would do its job, that you would in fact be perfectly comfortable. The point is that the impact of half a century of technology on the way in which you organise your daily lives is really relatively small.

There are a number of exceptions. Television has had a real impact, though I do not know how many of us would find its loss a serious deprivation. So has increased spatial mobility. But neither of these factors has made any really great difference to those at your income level. For those lower down the spectrum, the differences are much more marked, but they are due not so much to improved technology as to improved access to technology. The poor are not so poor. For the pace-setters like yourselves I can give you something like ten reasons, not necessarily in logical order, why I believe that the mass-effects of technology are going to be slower in coming than you imagine.

First, I believe — that is, I have a gut feeling — that there is a biological limitation to the acceptance of technology or to the acceptance of any sort of change at all. I think it is related to such constants as how long we take to grow up and how long we live, and that it is at least possible that we may be approaching this ultimate limit. We have now a very considerable amount of evidence from the developing countries, that to transform a village tribal chief living in a mud hut into a responsible civil servant simply cannot be done. The ethics, the motives, the way of life which would be involved in making this transition are apparently beyond the ability of the kind of people who find themselves in this situation. It took us probably some ten or twenty generations to get to this point. It seems to me totally unreasonable to expect it to happen in one generation irrespective of how much education you pump into the people involved. I have no reason to believe that the acceptance of major technological changes does not similarly require more than one generation.

My next group of delaying factors arise from what I regard as the unequivocally true fact that technology is the enemy of skill. I am quite sure that the change from carving an alabaster ashtray to moulding a plastic ashtray of imitation alabaster represents a very considerable loss of skill. Throughout history technology has on the whole acted in two directions, one, the reduction of physical labour, the other the reduction of the necessity for most people to have a moderate rate of skill and the substitution of the necessity for a smaller number of people to have a rather higher level of skill. I think we are perhaps at the beginning of a new age where technology, which over the last 5,000 years has been very largely concerned with the reduction of physical labour, will now be concerned chiefly with the abolition of intellectual activity. There is little doubt that the reduction of physical labour has been bad for our health; I do not know whether the abolition of intellectual activity will have similar negative side effects.

Technology as the antithesis of skill has had quite considerable social effects. As I have said, under simpler technologies everyone had to have a moderate level of skill. The newer technologies have much reduced this level, but make much greater intellectual demands on those who create and manipulate it. Thus technology accentuates the difference between the Few and the Many, and is essentially an anti-proletarian influence. Anybody can operate a pocket calculator, very few people can design one.

We have two choices as to how to deal with this accentuation of real differences. We can sidestep some of the effects by locking up the high technology in a separate bit of our society, and making it do work which has very little impact on the people as a whole. Basically that is what the Soviet Union has done; locking up its relatively small resources in the space programme and the weapon programme, and letting very little spill over into the population-wide consumer industries. This effectively limits the spread of technology. And so does the way we have chosen in the West. Our system seems likely to put the clock back and produce a resurgence of inherited property. At one time, the landowners and the coal-owners were in control of a large proportion of the resources of the nation, as often as not, by inheritance. If the ability to manipulate and create new technologies is going to be vested in a relatively small part of the population which has the intellectual ability to do so then it will become in some real sense inheritable. The occasional person will break through and work their way up, but this is something which has always happened. We are going to have a relatively small class who are going to be very powerful, by virtue of the fact that they have the intellectual training and equipment which allows them to manage this considerable resource. And we have to ask ourselves whether we can persuade these people, who will be responsible for creating and manufacturing a lot of the wealth which a country produces, to give of their talent and of their intellectual property sufficiently freely, without making excessive demands from the rest of society, either of power or of rewards. This is something which is against the spirit of the time — for one reason or another we believe it to be wrong, and I think that this too is a fairly powerful source of resistance to the spread of technology: we shall try to organise society in such a way as to at least postpone the day when this will happen.

There is of course a way of possibly sidestepping this problem, that is, to create 'The Replete Society' . . . This is a society where the productive capacity is such that everybody can have almost anything they like, and where therefore the institutionalised jealousy we call Socialism can be abolished. It will no longer be necessary to be jealous of anybody, because everybody can always have almost anything they like, certainly as far as material goods are concerned. Now, I think the Replete Society is attainable, but probably only by some fraction, which I am not clever enough to calculate, of the present world population. This might be an acceptable way of reaping the rewards of technology, without creating damaging social gradients, provided there was a big burst on the technology of population control. (This is one of the things my laboratory actually works on. There has been very little application of technology, apart from pharmacology, to the problems of population control. It has not been taken up in any field, so far as I know, which involves any of the other new technologies.)

Another damping effect on the future coming to pass as quickly as expected is what I call 'The Undemocraticising Effect' of high technology, the difficulty of putting the issues across to the population at large. I am very much depressed when people tell me that the majority of the population will not read more than 200 words at a go. The issues which one would like people to have some democratic opinion about such as nuclear power, are I think totally beyond the comprehension of the majority of the population.

So what are we to do? Start rolling dice to decide whether we're going to have a power station? Or say we are going to trust our MPs or Congressmen? I am certainly not going to say this. I think there is an increasing disenchantment with representatives talking for you at all levels, whether it is shop stewards, trade union officials, members of the Government, or members of Parliament. This delegation of powers of your own decision is something which I think on the whole people are rebelling against. But at the same time the issues are extremely difficult to understand and it is always safer for people who do not understand to say 'let's keep it the way it is at the moment; it seems to be working passably well'. This I think will prove to be another very powerful force which will damp down the introduction of new technologies.

The remedy may be to step up enormously our efforts to educate people, and make education a lifelong process. But the ability to comprehend may be lacking and it may not in fact be a question of simply pushing enough education out, so that this damping effect may well continue.

Connected with this is our ignorance in the realm of risk calculations. Very often a decision on the introduction of a new technology has to be made on the basis of the risks associated with it. All of us, whatever our education and intelligence, have non-linear scales of risk. It is very common for somebody to leap into their Ford Capri, with a slightly defective back brake and no safety belt, and to drive to the local hospital at sixty miles an hour in a thirty miles an hour limit area, to screech to a halt in the hospital car-park, to get out of the car, to pass through the doors of the hospital, and to suddenly expect to be ten thousand times as safe as before. His assessment of the risks to which he voluntarily exposes himself, and the risks which he allows other people to inflict upon him, work on quite different scales. I maintain that if nuclear radiation was blue and you could see it, it would be half the problem that it is. Because of its pervasive, invisible nature, people ascribe to it a risk factor quite out of proportion to the real risks involved.

So in addition to the general education of understanding what science and technology is about, I think we have to produce another form of education which actually gives people a realistic appreciation of risks and the choices involved. As far as I know this is totally unexplored. It is not taught in schools, it requires a knowledge of statistics, of trade offs, of being able to assess cumulative risks and very, very, very few members of the population have any sort of equipment for dealing with this situation. But those are the decisions which have to be made quite often when a new technology is in question.

This fear of risk has produced certain antibodies, for instance, Health and Safety legislation. Health and Safety legislation has nothing to do with health and safety. It is a way of putting a brake onto the introduction of new technology, which trade unions have, I think quite legitimately, exploited, perhaps to compensate them for their lessening power in the market-place. It has the enormous advantage that it takes a very courageous person indeed to say that to make this job or this operation safer, or healthier, is too expensive and should not be done. It is my view that Health and Safety legislation is used as a brake against technology. I do not think there is anything wrong with this; it is simply a legalised form of giving vent to innate conservatism.

It seems to me — though I have no evidence — that there are forces which keep the total amount of risk always about constant. On the one hand we are spending very considerable resources to reduce already improbable events of accident and health damage to make them even less probable. On the other hand, we use our whole advertising skill to sell risk to people — to go on ski-ing holidays, to mountaineer, to go surfing, and to buy faster motor cars. I have a theory that if I could persuade an industrial historian to investigate the total rate of death by accident from the beginning of the Industrial Revolution to now he might find that in fact it has remained roughly speaking constant. As we have reduced it in the workplace, we have introduced it into personal transport and we have deliberately made it part of our leisure activities. In fact we merchandise it, we market it in order to fulfil what is apparently some kind of desire.

My next damping effect I call 'The Management of the Dissident Minority'.

A historian in the year 5,000 describing our different forms of govenment, would I think find that the descriptor with the greatest power of distinguishing between different forms of government was how they managed the dissidents, the very small proportion of the population who would not play the game. Do you shoot them? Do you have very large police forces; do you have police computers; do you lock them up in Siberia; do you rehabilitate them in special open prisons? The way this problem is managed is I think the label of a culture and a form of government. I believe this is important to our present argument because the technology of centralisation steadily reduces the number of dissidents required to produce a very substantial effect on society. People living in a village economy can be almost as dissident as they like, because their impact on the population at large is very small. If on the other hand you have only one huge nuclear power station in a country, it does not take very many people to effect a very serious disruption. We all know that you only have to pick up a telephone and say 'I've just put a bomb in Selfridges in Oxford Street', to mobilise hundreds of policemen, and bring the life of a part of London to a halt.

So I think again we have a choice: technology can take one of two paths. It can continue to chase the alleged economies of scale, making things very big and very centralised, and accept the danger of having to manage dissident minorities with increasing ferocity, we would have to take more precautions, have more guards, more security systems, because of the vulnerability of the centralised systems, and this could dominate the whole society. The alternative is to distribute technology. I have no doubt it would be possible to have nuclear power-packs to produce electric power for a block of flats, sealed and working for ten years at a time, with a flexible servicing interval. This would decentralise an important facility, and, because no draconian measures would be required to protect it, would have a stabilising effect on society.

This is a special case of the problem of coping with people who by some non-democratic means have acquired the power to paralyse appreciable parts of society. We should avoid putting people into this position because we do not know how to manage them. The dispersal of important resources is therefore to my mind a very severe and very necessary challenge which ought to be put to purveyors of technology. In a small way it has already happened. I am quite sure that after every electricity strike, the shares of firms making petrol generators boom, as more people find it worthwhile to tie up an appreciable amount of capital in making themselves independent of a centralised service. If I was running a very large corporation, I would set my corporate planners looking at the technology of independence.

Man became civilised when he ceased having to find the food he wanted to eat each separate day. When he learned to store things in barns he had some leisure time, and he could do the sort of things which we call civilisation or culture. We have regressed and are increasingly reduced to the hand-to-mouth kind of existence early Man had, because we are so dependent on the electricity supply working, and the gas supply working, and the petrol in the garage not drying up — things you need supplied almost continuously. We can easily lose the security which for a time civilised Man enjoyed, by having at least his short-term needs under his own control.

This seems to me to be the real parting of the ways for the

large-scale technological planner. If he decides to go for large centralised systems, this itself will act as a brake. The disruption can be caused by dissident minorities or by people who have got undemocratic control of the facility, and could hold back the way in which technology is deployed.

My next factor arises from a theorem 'The lowest cost society would be that which will keep the largest proportion of its population at work.' This is of course the exact opposite of what we are presently trying to do. The factories of the future now seem likely to be big black boxes with the raw materials going in at one end, and the finished product coming out at the other end, only requiring a few clever people to work the computers and a slightly larger number of clever people to work the computers and a slightly larger number of clever people to make the robots in the first place. This would have a devastating effect on employment, and it could be made to come true. But this must be set against the fact that all Western societies, and Eastern Bloc societies as well, are pretty firmly wedded to the concept that you do not actually have people starving in the streets. Everybody, regardless of whether they work or not, gets something like a living wage. We have the choice of whether we pay it for doing something or for not doing anything.

I would maintain that if technology is wantonly used for job-destruction (at no real saving to society since people will have to be kept eating anyway), then the extra cost of dissidents and restrictive practices added to the actual cost of Social Security, will be higher than doing the same tasks apparently less efficiently by keeping the people at work. This of course is the basis of a great deal of trade union objection to the introduction of new processes, and I think they are right. Unless it can be demonstrated that employment will be found for them somewhere else, it is crazy to take people out of employment and make them unhappy and dissident, for an illusory saving in resources.

Thus whenever anybody introduces a 'labour-saving' technology, it must be done by offering alternative forms of employment, say in the Care Industry, or the Education Industry, both of which are labour-intensive. Otherwise it seems to me that an increase in overall wealth is more likely to be produced by a decrease in the introduction of technology than by its increase.

And finally, two perhaps disconnected concepts. A lot is said about the benefits of communications technology, in making a lot of information available in the home and being able to communicate with anybody you like. I do not know what evidence the purveyors of this concept have that anybody actually wants this. In the early nineteen sixties, I was concerned with the introduction of electronics into the intensive care ward in hospitals. It became possible to monitor a number of important physiological variables, and to display them on cathode ray tube screens. However, I found I had to impress on the people working for me the big difference between monitoring and measuring, which to my mind had at that time always been confused. Measuring occurs when somebody is sufficiently interested to walk up to the display device and take a reading: it requires motivation on the part of the enquirer. Monitoring actually shouts at you, whether you want to know the information or not, it does not rely on your motivation to enquire, but actually screams at you, 'Look, look at me — I have something to communicate to you'.

Now when people assume that the very ready acceptance of television will be transferred to availability of hundreds of thousands of pages of information which a new communication technology will give us, I think they suffer from exactly the same confusion. Television programmes are essentially undemanding, the watcher is the recipient of something that is being pushed out at him essentially similar to advertising; it is like a monitoring system, it shouts at you.

The large-scale availability of information, on the other hand, will only be of use to those who are prepared to take the initiative. It will be like going to the public library to look something up. You have to find the right page of *Prestel* in order to find what you may be looking for, and this presupposes that you actually have the motivation. I think that if you were to compare the number of people who are compulsive viewers of television with the number of people who make regular use of the reference section of public libraries, you would find there was a very large numerical difference.

The last thing I want to talk about is what I call the technology of deterrence. We may find ourselves in a situation where we have shown that a thing is possible, but we decide not to use it. We have shown that the hydrogen bomb is possible, but so far the principle of deterrence has worked, and we haven't actually dropped hydrogen bombs on anyone. Are people going to spend a lot of money inventing and developing a technology then finding that they cannot use it? This I think is also going to be an interesting braking phenomenon.

I have tried to demonstrate to you my *belief* — with no real evidence — that there is a tendency to overestimate the rapidity with which technology will actually change our society. There is still time to make real choices — for instance the choice between the technology of independence and the technology of centralisation.

PART THREE
Introduction

To state that science speculation and science fiction are democratic activities does not imply that the two are necessarily the same. The first is subject to rules, even if the rules differ according to the type of speculation that its authors undertake. The second is only limited by the imagination of the author, his abilities and his powers of persuasion. (For him, read her throughout.) Which means that whatever school of science fiction the writers are seen as being involved with, hard technology centered, science fantasy, future history, their output will differ in aim and intention.

What first follows are two pieces by well known science fiction writers, writers who, off the page and away from their imaginative constructs, could not be more different. Yet both are, each in his own way, deeply immersed in philosophy, a characteristic which many of science fiction's successes can not help but share.

However, they still approach the world differently. Both have weird, in the old fashioned sense of the term, imaginations. But then this is no more than to be expected: to live in and with an imagination which will make your living does tend to indicate that it will differ from most of the rest of humanities. Anyone who can, as does A. E. Van Vogt, postulate an intelligent decision-making particle is obviously different from the rest of us.

Yes, both authors are very different, even down to physical differences. And the pieces convey those differences. I tried to dismiss from my mind their physical reality, and imagine what they might look like, strictly from the material on the written page. I visualised Harry Harrison as a small, energetic, bustling and battling personality, one who speaks at twice the rate of the rest of us. And A. E. Van Vogt, an almost phlegmatic, tall, think before you speak Lone Ranger, a sort of James Stewart in cowboy rig.

This, with a couple of additions, was exactly right. To Harry Harrison you add a grey, pointed gnomish beard and a red shirt. to A. E. Van Vogt a business suit and glasses.

It will quickly become apparent from either of them that to be a science fiction writer is at least a craft, one which requires study, thought, and in which experience helps. Now it may be that science fiction is the best selling form of literature that there is, it is however also possible that more people get their ideas of science fiction from the movies and from television than ever get it from books.

So how does Hollywood, a short-hand term for the world's movie and television industry, treat science fiction subjects? The history as Suzanne Landa shows in her short tour through science fiction movies of the past is not a particularly happy one — views with which Harry Harrison would agree.

Why this should be so would take up an essay in itself, though some clues are to be found in our exercise in television series creation. Once again we are in the territory of the old ever-with-us argument between the specialist and the generalist, the first believing that the other can never get it right, the second that specialists will not be able to create for a general audience.

I include the exercise here because it is fun. Not too much

should be read into it. Nobody goes so far as to state that this is how the germs of ideas for television series are arrived at, though sometimes looking at the results one should not be surprised if they were. And, as will become quickly apparent, it became dominated by people with television and film expertise who perhaps had sat in on too many exercises like this.

5   INVENTING NEW WORLDS I

H. Harrison

> *Harry Harrison has had over 50 books published and has edited*
> *almost countless anthologies. His best known books are* Deathworld
> *which* The Times Literary Supplement *listed as one of the best 50*
> *American novels of the 1950s, and* Make Room! Make Room!
> *which became the film 'Soylent Green'.*

I am a science fiction writer — a highly skilled profession.
I will be pointing out some of the profession's peaks and
some of the depths. And I will be telling you what science
fiction is. What we do not need, however, are more of the
academic approaches to science fiction — which in case you
did not know is a very big industry in the United States at
the college level. There are people teaching science fiction, to
people teaching science fiction to people teaching science fiction. So like anthropologists, teaching anthropology to anthropologists. And we do not need those either. But let me establish what we are talking about. We are discussing the relation
between science fact and science fantasy. There are a number
of different definitions of science fiction — none of which
work. The only method that really works is to point at something and call it science fiction. But there is a way of
representing this graphically. This is a circle which holds all
of world fiction. A great big field of fiction where you make
things up. Somewhere in there is also fantasy. The problem
is to distinguish between the two. It is not too difficult

because science fiction is right in the middle of fantasy. In the centre of science fiction is the stuff you recognise as SCIENCE fiction. Dear old Arthur Clarke is in there, with carbon filaments up to the satellites. Bob Heinlein is in there. You know what that is. What gives you a problem with science fiction is Ray Bradbury. He has one foot in fantasy, and the other foot in science fiction. I belong to a rather small minority of people in the centre, who care about science and deal with science in a fictional form. Now it sounds hard to do and it is. If you want an example, I will mention one of my own books, a book called *Make Room, Make Room*, which I wrote far too long ago. It was written at a time when there were no popular books about population. I did a bit of work — three, four, five years of research. And I wrote this novel in a world not generated by me. I used everybody else's facts. I used the worst case scenario. This is what science fiction does; it shakes the admonitory finger. Shape up or this is what you can expect. I set this world and put a story in it that does not even mention the world until about the eightieth page. This is hard science fiction. You cannot fault it. The figures? I got some from the petroleum council, they told me how much they had in the ground. I got more figures from the Malthus people, they told me how many people were being born every day.

Somebody asked me for titles of books that are good science fiction. And I had to say very quickly that most science fiction is pretty crappy. We talk in science fiction about Sturgeon's Law, discovered by Ted Sturgeon, a science fiction writer of note. When somebody said, 'Ah, I don't read science fiction, 90 per cent of it is crap', he said, 'Ninety per cent of all fiction is crap'. And that is very true. If you are going to judge the romance novel, which is very popular, you do not judge it by the boobs and bottoms. It is Elisabeth Jane Howard you are talking about, and she doesn't say 'Oh my romance novel is crap'. Science fiction has this residue, well no, this cream at the top, pardon me, of really good books. Unhappily, it is not getting proper academic attention; not, I quickly add, the kind of attention that Dr. Cort gives it. He is a historian of science fiction. That we can use.

In the United States the academic machine is grinding out Ph.Ds. and they have gone into science fiction. A few years ago some academics had a meeting at Stanford, and they invited some science fiction writers to come and talk. Up there on the platform, the guy ahead of me was a Professor of astronautics — not bad. The guy that came after me was a chemist. What is this? The guy knew science fiction and talked about it. I asked the fellow running the meeting 'Where is your English department?' 'They would not come here, they would not think about science fiction, they have to have the text laid out.' Well that was a long time ago. The texts are now laid out. They have a few favourite writers. They deal with the same writers all the time, people like Rogers Lasney, Chip DeLaney, two very nice guys. But, Jim Blishford, Lasney and DeLaney substitute myth for plot: plot is better. The Professors like that. I hate to be anti-academic, because I appreciate what the right people are doing, there is a place for science fiction in the schools, in the middle level. There are about, the last I knew, over two thousand classes in schools, grammar schools, in science fiction. Ha, you laugh, ha ha ha, what's it doing in schools? It's a tool. The teachers teach it because the children voluntarily read the books. There is no other art that you can say that about. I took a lot of these classes. I told the class I would write a textbook about it. They use it. These children are not what you think. They're one-third or one quarter of the bright-eyed kids who rattle off stuff anyway. The other three-quarters are under-achievers, poor students: the

teachers utilise science fiction as a tool to get access to reading skills, scientific skills, logical skills and this sort of thing.
I appreciate that. I do not appreciate the people who are
using it for one more Ph.D. thesis.

Brian Aldiss said once, after this whole thing had started,
'Let's get science fiction out of the classroom back in the
gutter where it belongs.' So you might say I'm a gutter
writer.

The science fiction in the centre of that circle is what I
want to talk about. The science fiction in the centre of that
circle is one man or woman's view of a particular reality
which he creates. Years ago, in his book *New Maps of Hell*,
Kingsley Amis said 'science fiction is written by English and
American men', not that women are foreigners. There was a
little bit of truth in that, though not too much. Science fiction, that stuff in the centre, has a residue, a complete lack of
worry about the continuity of science. Most science is concerned with step by step progression. When you are writing
science fiction, the science content can be very limited and
very extrapolative — which is where it goes away from
futurism. A lot of science fiction writers are futurists. I was
for a long time. But futurism is like science in that it is linear.
It's a progression, one by one by one. The Delphi programmes, which a lot of people rely on, are not predicting,
really. The predictions brought out by Delphites were never
followed up ten years later to see what had happened. I do
not think they are any more responsible than the linear predictions, the science of the futurists, when all of the big
explosive events of our time in science, were not predicted
by the scientists (though at least two or three were predicted by A. E. Van Vogt). You couldn't get the transistor
out of linear science. It's a jump aside.

What science fiction is doing then, again the good stuff
in the centre, is entertaining. It has to be entertaining because

it's the thinking man's garbage, the thinking man's entertainment. Paul Anderson said that when he writes a book, he is fighting for a six-pack of beer. A guy goes out, money in his pocket. Will he buy a six-pack or a paperback? Hopefully he'll buy the paperback. I'd buy the six-pack of beer, myself.

We do not invent new worlds. We apply what we know, we apply what we think we know, we apply art to the hard facts of science in the centre. That's it, we're artists. Don't ask too much of us. We'll write, but we may not know what we are writing. In one of Van Vogt's books, I think it was *The World of Null-A*, he has a chap talking to a small, black box on a table, which has a memory in it. He asks it to plan the city and give advice. It's a little mini-computer or something. He was criticised by Damon Knight, saying that, 'The man is wrong. Why do you waste your technology. That memory, impossible to get that into a small box'. Now who was right, Damon or Van? The chip came along, which was not predicted. The chip came out of another technology. We never saw it. But the science fiction writers with this openness, this approach, did do a certain amount of prediction. I hate to use the word prediction. We do not predict, if anything, science fiction shot-guns the future. A lot of our ideas go out. After it is all over, it is like astrology. You always remember the one that worked.

We come out of the gutter and there are times we are going back into the gutter. Early science fiction is just crap. In early science fiction, there is one very nice story about a petrol driven rocket, going to Mars, bang bang bang bang all the way over there. I forget how they justify it, where they get enough oxygen from. But no one seemed to mind it very much. It really is boy's science fiction. The man who invented modern science fiction, whose name should be remembered, is John W. Campbell, and he trained as a physicist. He took this rather amorphous field of fantasy, which was just sound and fury and noise, and he turned it into this bit of inspiration which a lot of people read. I recall my mother saying, 'Reading that garbage, what do you do with it?' I grew up to write garbage, that is what I did with it. But not all of us are privileged to be able to write garbage and get paid for it.

Science fiction is *different*. We are asking for a difference. Science fiction shares with science the future. Any scientific process, any experiment always ends in the future. It goes into the future, if you want to try and guess how it ends, you guess, you speculate, you experiment and it doesn't work. Back to the drawing board. Science fiction ends in the future. Science fiction is the only sort of fiction that, like science, knows the future exists. In a modern historical novel, everybody deals in the past. They deal with inter-personal relationships. Take out the cars of any novel today and put in buggies, take out the planes and put in ships, and it would not affect the real worth of the novel in the slightest.

Science fiction, like science, will admit that the future exists. And, it will do an even more important thing, it will admit that there is change. And, a final thing it will do is to admit that you can change change. And that is what research is about, this is what scientific thinking is about, and this is what science fiction is about. When you read a decent science fiction book, you are getting back from it. You are getting something that the writer with a particular thing put into it. Maybe, it may come out subconsciously, I do not know. You read Arthur Clarke's novels for instance and there is not a human being in them. They turn sideways, absolutely invisible.

But when you go up there to the moon, full of moon-dust, ah, even though he is wrong about the moon, he is right about the novel. When you go through *Rendezvous with Rama*, it an absolutely non-interpersonal relationship book.

I do not remember the names of the characters, I do not remember what positions they held or who they were, I do not even remember the name of the ship's captain. What they did was go out and explore this fantastic artefact. And in there they build up to the discovery which is what the book is really about — it is a lot of fun — the mechanics about seeing that artefact in space, and finding out and exploring it. The book is a great big simple statement that you can not argue with until he proves it. The statement is that the only way you can transmit information over light years is with genes. It is not a new idea in science fiction. But it is a new idea to the general public. There is no other way. There is no metal, there is no way of preserving any material except in repeating it like a gene that will do it all over again. He has these machines there. You read the book and you are convinced. I re-read it a few months ago, and it convinced me again. Hard core technology science fiction. It has a place in life, aside from the entertainment value. If it was just entertainment, I would not be here.

It has got to the point now where science fiction speaks across the ages and speaks across the languages, as an international science fiction. Whatever the thing is, that special thing in science fiction is something new in the world. Now, I know we all brag a lot about new things, but it is the literature of the twentieth century. The first science fiction writer was not Jules Verne. Jules Verne was a rotten scientist: he recycled a lot of the current bad theories about science. His books are great boy's adventures. They are good stuff, they are history — in the history of science fiction, but unrealistic — like firing off a shell with four guys and a dog in it. The acceleration was not enough. It would have gone about three miles and then it would have dropped back, but there was enough acceleration to make them all red pulp in the bottom. It's a great book!

The first science fiction writer was H. G. Wells whose first book was written in 1898, *The Time Machine*. He had two or three things going for him, he knew his science, he also knew how to write. That has not caught up with a lot of people yet in science fiction. We are running on Wells' coattails. He did invent a number of devices that we are still recapitulating. We got Wells, and had an awareness of the machine age. I have heard a lot of things mostly from American Professors about the myths of the machine age of science fiction. I do not think this is so. I think science fiction deals with the age we live in, which is a machine age and is aware of the fact that science has changed every facet of our life.

It (science fiction) is becoming adult now. There is characterisation. People like Narry Niven write classic science fiction in a sense that the hero is an idea. Only in science fiction do you have the gadget or the machine or the idea as hero. If the gadget is the hero, you do not need anybody in the story, do you? I have written very, very good stories, with nobody in them. One is about an intergalactic probe. The machine was sent up and rattled away for about two million years. You follow the probe and it comes back to earth and the earth is gone. It takes a look and goes away again. That's a nice idea.

The soft sciences came into science fiction in the 1950s with a magazine called *Galaxy*, edited by Horace Gold. Up to that point science fiction was physics and chemistry and things that came out of them: aeronautics, astronautics, great rockets, time machines, warps. He brought in the other sciences of philosophy, psychology, and the interesting things that make people tick. And that either corrupted or improved science fiction, depending on your point of view. I think it improved it.

A. E. Van Vogt

A. E. Van Vogt had his first story published in 1934 and his first science fiction story published in 1939. He has written many science fiction books, the best known of which are probably The World of Null A *and* Slan.*.*

All my life I have been what is called a square. A very serious type of person. A slow thinker. I am one of those odd types who, lacking natural talent and having no natural intuition — these are probably related phenomena — had to *think* my way through life.

I worked out a system for writing. When I tell that to people they feel kind of stunned. My method of writing is probably different from that of other writers. I have no advance outline. In fact I couldn't make one up. But none the less I use a systematic approach. But each new development in the plot, while implicit in the previous material, is as much of a surprise to me as I hope it will be to the reader.

The very first story I wrote, I wrote in 800 word scenes with five steps in each scene. It was about 9,000 words long and therefore it had about 1,000 sentences and each one of those sentences had emotion in it. One thousand sentences of emotion. It sold on the basis of that. Subsequently I decided that science fiction needed a hang-up in every sentence. That is, it had to have a thing in it where the reader made a contribution. Years later I read *Understanding Media* by McLuhan and I discovered that he had a word for that kind of thing, it was 'hot fiction', like radio where the listener has to contribute a picture.

He gets the message through his ears. I require from the science fiction reader in other senses a contribution so that he makes up a picture of what I am trying to describe to him. When I describe an alien, this creature that had just come in, whatever it was 'reaches inside a fold of its skin', what seemed to be a fold of its skin (there we have the hang-up!) and 'drew out a tiny silver object'. We do not know what that silver object is. We could suspect that it is a weapon but when he points it at us it speaks. Each sentence explains a little of what happened before but meanwhile we don't know what it means now. I discovered you can't do that with every one of a thousand sentences! Currently, storywise, I am, in my slow fashion, considering what the universe would be like if an anti-baryon readjustment took place.

Now, you can see already that that is a high level consideration. It has nothing to do with the human race because the human race would not exist if an anti-baryon readjustment took place. This has to do with that host of new particles that are showing up in the studies of physics and so on. A world in which anti-baryons had been balanced with baryons is a feat of imagination.

Now such a world as an anti-baryon readjustment probably comes under the heading of inventing new worlds, or indeed even a new universe. Most science fiction does not operate at that level of invention. You probably know that we operate at the level of picking an aspect of some potential social change and asking ourselves what would happen if that took place. A story about such an option, if it is entertaining, gives us a chance to consider in three or four hours what in real life — if it happened — would be enforced upon us every day for forty to seventy years. The violent idealists who set up new systems, and their cunning pragmatic heirs, normally enforce their systems far beyond the time when it is apparent to onlookers that the thing is not producing what was promised.

The second type of inventing new worlds is more literal. And, in connection with that I should like to refer to a letter I sent out about a year ago, to approximately 450 science fiction writers all over the world. The letter began with three headings: 'The Meaning of Life'; 'The Meaning of the Universe'; 'Has Science Fiction given Any Clues'.

Further along in the letter was another heading: 'The Search for New Sciences in Science Fiction'. Under that heading I wrote: 'What I probably really mean is subsciences.'

The science fiction writers, it turned out, didn't regard themselves as innovators. That really surprised me. Arthur C. Clarke who is responsible for those fixed orbit ideas, wrote, 'I can't think of a thing that I ever did.' A few years ago a famous scientist told me that an idea of mine, in my novel *Mission to the Stars* had started him thinking. Could that be done? — he asked himself. It turned out that it could and it worked. That is on the level of research.

Without exception, the writers who were scientists, or had science degrees, disavowed *any* original scientific contribution of any kind. Most of the so-called New Wave writers did not even answer. Frank Herbert phoned and described two of his science fiction inventions that were in production. One had to do with the television system he had aboard his submarine. Joe Haldeman sent me a marked copy of his novel, *Planet of Judgement* about a new science, *arivne*, which has to do with foretelling the future. Some time later, when I personally asked one of the writers (who had a degree in physics) why he did not regard his many unique science fictional scientific concepts as candidates for a sub-science, he was tolerant. There were no new sciences, he pointed out — and never could be. Physics and chemistry between them covered the interactions of matter and energy, such aspects of physics as electronics were merely engineering applications.

Similarly, most events in space would come under the heading of Astronomy. Thus the entire application of the known sciences to human beings occupying a planet with a different atmosphere, gravity and ecology were again engineering problems.

There is a great deal of truth in such exact definitions. But I don't buy it. The final evidence about the nature of the universe is not in yet. It could be that in physics and chemistry we are looking at, yes, some very stable aspects. But there may be a more basic science involved.

Meanwhile, I accept the more limited view. It's practical. It fits the moment by moment life we seem to be living. None the less, there are some interesting engineering possibilities ahead. Here in the solar system we can look forward to a score of special situations, for which I herewith tentatively invent the following names: Moon Mission; Mars Landing; Venus Control; Mercury Outpost; Jupiter Station One; Jupiter Station Two; Jupiter Station Three; Saturn Ring Operations and Solar Distance Studies (Neptune, Uranus, Pluto).

We are already acquiring special names for the space orbiting conditions, and space manufacturing complexes. The word 'meteorite mining' for the Asteroid belt does not seem an adequate description.

Most of the worlds that I have invented by my various systems grow out of the current problems of the world. Thus, in *The Anarchistic Colossus*, I invented the technology that would be required for anarchism to work. I foresaw no change in human nature so technology would have to do the whole job.

Similarly in *The World of Null-A*, I envisaged a new world of the future in which Korzbyski's General Semantics made it possible for people to live without government but this time, the person had to take training and was tested by a monster computer called the 'Games Machine'. If he was successful he was allowed to live on Non-Aristotelian Venus with other people who had passed the tests given by the Games Machine.

You'll notice that neither of these invented worlds accepted that an average man, conditioned by his parents, friends, and teachers was qualified for a stateless society.

Approximately the same problem is solved in *The Weapon Shop* stories. But there the method is that you can obtain from the weapon makers a defensive gun — actually it's a particle accelerator. It's a term I didn't know at that time but that is what it is. When they drew that, they were using a particle accelerator of some kind which would only discharge if you used it to defend yourself. Now just imagine the kind of particle that would be needed to establish that this was a defensive situation. That is what we are going to have to look forward to at some future time, and I trust that these particles that are coming up will do the job with great skill.

As the years went by, after I finished the *World of Null-A*, it developed that Venus was a planet with surface temperature somewhat too high to support human life. Somewhat too high! So, in doing a revision ten or so years ago, I explained that somewhere in the twenty-second century ice meteors were towed from the Saturn rings — this would come under the heading of being a Saturn Ring Operation — and put into close orbit around Venus. So that, eventually, as the huge meteors (some of them 100 cubic mile masses) hit the atmosphere they began to melt, and it began to rain. It did not just rain 40 days and nights, but 4,000 days and nights. And when that rain had washed the atmosphere closer to the surface there were huge oceans, an oxygen atmosphere and a whole new, invented Venus, which could now fit what I had on The World of Null-A.

I was very pleased with that invention and I really think it could be done. But, amazingly, science is moving so rapidly that there is a fabulous new idea for, so to speak, salting the atmosphere of Venus with a small life form, which feeds on the gasses in the upper atmosphere of that strange planet. The prediction is that 90 per cent of the atmosphere will eventually fall automatically. And in twenty years, Venus could have huge oceans, ample oxygen and be suitable for human habitation.

At the moment both my ice meteor and the virus injection idea qualify as methods for inventing new worlds, because that would really be a wonderful new world. This is in the gist of the answer that Philip Jose Farmer sent in response to my letter. He described a planet that he had invented for a novel of his. Farmer felt that he had worked out the conditions of that planet within the frame of creating a new sub-science.

So there we have the two most often used methods of inventing new worlds in science fiction: one the future option, the other a planet different from earth whereby we are given a reasonably worked out scientifically accurate description of how it would be. The best writers for this second level of invention are those who are scientifically trained. I am not, by the way: I know something about science, I would say, but I have never been scientifically trained in the proper meaning of that term.

There is another thing going on as a result of science fiction. The writing and reading of science fiction is expanding the consciousness of those involved. Arthur C. Clarke wrote, as I say, saying that he couldn't think of a single, new sub-science he had invented in his science fiction. Yet, he came up with that fixed orbit idea. What I think happened is that reading and writing science fiction created a new Arthur C. Clarke. I feel as if over the years I have been created, developed, and expanded a number of times.

7 BRAIN STORM:
Or how not to write a Sci-fi Movie . . .

The discussion was heated, at times acrymonious, and sometimes almost libellous. It was led by a leading Hollywood television script writer, and after reading it you can easily understand why he wishes to remain anonymous.

It began as an exercise: how would you write a sci-fi television movie? He picked as our starting point the existence of the television series, Buck Rogers, an up date of a famous cartoon character strip of the thirties.

As ever, there was no way in which a collection of rampant egos could be confined to Buck Rogers or anything else. And they were not. In passing there was an onslaught, shared almost entirely by all those who could manage to sidle a word in, on the ethos of Hollywood, and how it manages to screw up science fiction.

I am one of the dreaded television writers, not an artist, and I am toiling in commercial television. Our primary function is to create a popular show, usually aimed at the lowest common denominator. Get the ratings and satisfy the sponsors, so that you keep getting the money in. People in our industry, I think, are beginning to look on space as the new Western or the new Spy device. I think that is true but it is also I think fertile ground for just about any genre. And when we started talking about the episodic part of Buck Rogers, we decided that the best way to approach it would be to deal with prototype stories in classic form. Work out the plot then fill in the science fiction as we go, with emphasis on human conflict rather than the technology being the villain, we will find that the humans are the villains, and Buck is always the hero, naturally who comes to the rescue. He is really a James Bond in the twenty-fifth century. He's not the one that we knew in the thirties. He is one of the twentieth century astronauts left in a time warp and he returns in the twenty-fifth century. He comes back in time to save the earth from the Draconian empire which is sending a giant mother-ship to invade it. He does it by being able to improvise and innovate, whereas the people in the twenty-fifth century have to confer with their computers before they decide what to do. The computers are not actually the government but there is a panel of advisers, something like the Supreme Court, the humans do not really want to make any mistakes and the computers are, if not infallible, all knowing. The earth in the context of the series is basically desolate. There has been the inevitable atomic holocaust, and, except for the unfortunate few, everyone lives in controlled environments. Pre-holocaust history is forbidden and there are earth colonies throughout the universe. Apparently, some time before the holocaust humans got out and began to colonise. Some are still friendly, others are hostile and thereby comes the conflict. And how they travel to these distant galaxies within the context of an hour episode is not really worked out, but they do it.

You would need at least a week between each galaxy . . .

No, actually they usually do it within fifteen minutes. In fact one of the things we toyed with was a thing called a 'Stargate' (as in 'Star Wars' when Solo blasts through) but, as you probably realise on television there are tremendous budget constraints. So 'Stargating' is out. So we just simply cut, and there they are . . .

Here is the situation:
A planetoid, from a distant galaxy, which as we will find out in our initial probe, has a friendly atmosphere, somehow orbits earth in 1985, or perhaps get into a geosynchronous orbit around the sun. So that the technology that we still have, the one that fails to cope with the internal combustion engine, for example, has a certain opportunity to analyse, explore and exploit a totally new world, a real frontier which we can look out of the window and actually see. So, that's the situation and I wonder if anyone would speculate on what might happen. Take it from there.

Make it a quarter of a mile, 500 feet in diameter and give it an earth orbit, right?

Well, let's think TV, OK. Let's think big enough that time on the planet could be a factor. In other words it's earth-like.

It could not be earth like, because if it has been drifting through space: it has had less sun.

Well, let's say some distant intelligence that we don't know about. Its sun was going out and they built this. They had the technology to build it and send it off to another world that eventually they would be able to take over. And now, . . .

We are busy, we do not want it. We do not want Boat People, we do not want planetoids. They are the wrong colour.

But they are not necessarily there. They could have died in transit.

Could you not just have it as an empty box careering through space, a carved out meteorite, say? It would cut down on extras.

But where are the rocks and the trees?

Well, you see rocks and trees are not allowed.

To really cut down on the budget it should really be a giant replica of the BBC Television Centre. We would have no trouble with sets.

It's the size of Madagascar, roughly speaking, and it has some material inside it which is sufficiently dense to have some gravity, much smaller than Earth's of course, you have to do something to keep the atmosphere there.

Could an atmosphere be artificially created?

But it would not stay if there was no gravity. You would have to live on the inside. You would have to have some gravity. It has to be far enough away not to have tidal effects.

Bang! Splash in the Atlantic Ocean. Tidal waves. Japanese buildings going down . . . or hands sticking out of the water. You pick up the publicity from Skylab, right? O.K., hits the water. There it is floating around. It is alive. There are people inside it. There are things coming out of it. Week after week they come out. They go back in. Battleships, you fly planes, you bomb it, you lob stuff. The hell with space, y'know. That's it, get it down there and you gotta have something in the water. You got surfboards going in. But keep it simple. You land the thing. Bang. Right down. That makes life simple.

This man has dealt with networks before, you must have, haven't you?

Budget, always think budget.

But you see what happens is that the network discards that because it would be categorized as crap.

Having been exposed to television all my life, how could they tell?

Send it to a holiday resort.

Right. Hit Butlins. Whango, like that. Hit Blackpool, land on top of the tower. Take out Washington. Take out

New York. No one likes New York. It lands on top of Manhattan Island. Squash.

If it landed in New York, no one would notice. They would walk around and step right over it.

Or they would try to sell it or buy it.

They would try to move it to Atlantic City into a casino.

They might notice it. I think you've got to land the thing, really.

Is it dangerous?

There's a scramble for the goodies, OK you have the Russians, you have the Chinese, and would there be private people?

You could use it for advertising. Just put a big billboard up in front of it.

It is not that close. It's going to have to be a pretty big billboard.

The space shuttle could be taken over, and then as it comes back to ground it's got your alien beasts on board.

Let's do it in reverse. Let's send people up to look at it and they don't come back. There's two possibilities: one, that the hostile aliens have eaten them, and two, that there's a hell of a party going on.

They go up, they don't come back, the Americans immediately say that the Russians have got them. The Russians have got in there first. There are challenges and counter-challenges on either side. They very rapidly go to an exchange of missiles. You have the Third World War. Humanity is almost entirely wiped out and you end with Jimmy Carter in some citadel in the remnants of New York, or should it be Washington?, telling the world that they are going to start again. Well, you start with a completely Americanised world, with all ten inhabitants saluting the flag and saying, 'Now we will find out what is up there.'

What if you took those ten guys and put them up on that

planet? Is that what would happen? An Americanised society? Would they go up there and make all the same mistakes that we have made here?

You have a real problem. You are taking only ten guys and you put them on a thing like that and they are autonomous. They are up there and they can drop things on us and they are immediately a threat and you have a colony which might be hostile, so you have a world concern to control the colony which you put in a very powerful position.

We have had this before, you know, and it was known as the Roman Carthaginian war. There were Carthaginians over there they did not like and the Romans had to go and wipe them out. It would mean simply a repeat, a rerun of human history.

Would it?

Yes.

Given what we have in 1985?

Well, I do not think what we are going to have in 1985 is going to make it any better than what we have today. I think we are going to be just as nasty with the people who come from outer space as we are being nasty with each other. I admire the frequent optimism I have been listening to. I think you all have lived with television too long. You ought to join the human race.

Pessimism does not sell.

Change it to 1999, it's a good year, the millenia. Say there's only one guy aboard. And he's got a big white beard and long robes and he says, 'Well this is it kid. If you are waiting for me, I am here now.'

He comes in, and this thing appears and on it there is this being who knows a lot of things that we do not know. And we have a real problem as to whether we are going to let him say anything or whether we are going to shut him up fast, because we do not want to know all the answers. They are nasty.

What if the Chinese got to him first? What would they do?
What if he's black and hunchback and Jewish?

You might cover the ratings pretty well.

No, he is very, very good. He's so good that he is a real
big threat. Anybody like that standing up, would be trouble.

How about this scenario?:

A fairly big earthquake, and a sizeable island appears in
the middle of the Pacific, which may or may not be found to
be full of Manganese modules, or something of this kind, it's
an unclaimed habitable territory, and what would we do
about claiming it?

No, it seems to me that if it came from somewhere else
you might have other alloys, possibly. Things that we are
running out of for example, maybe it's made of petroleum,
or coal, or metal.

This great big satellite comes by, a hundred miles in
diameter, goes in an earth orbit, it is pure petroleum. There
it is, and there is interest. Up we go, who owns that thing?

Yes, that's the question. Let's forget for a minute what
happens up there, what happens down here, does the UN get
together and say, we are going to share it, or what?

Anything like that, if it was made of diamonds or gold, it
would be a ruinous threat to a certain kind of industry,
even if it was something terribly desirable. There are very
few things that we really want, but the scarcer they are, the
less we want them to arrive in lumps.

Egg of an alien beast, there is pulp to fry. You can eat it;
take bits of it down and save Africa. . . .

Say it was manna. Say it was made of a sort of a food,
totally renewable food, so that nobody ever had to work
for food again.

Every person that goes there, picks up some vitamin or
virus or something that automatically increases their intelli-

gence 500-fold, and they just do not want to come back. Every time we send an investigator out it just goes very quiet. What do we do eventually after we have several hundred people up there, who just do not say anything and do not want to return?

If you have several hundred people up there and they are that smart, they are probably taking over by then.

Let us go back to the edible one. The edible one was good, think of the sponsors that way. If it is cornflakes, you get a great big bowl of cornflakes.

But if they are up there mucking around on it, who is going to want to eat it?

Everyone must have cornflakes.

We have a great thing up there. Now what?

Well, we do not know. We, the proverbial network bigwigs, do not know what we are going to find up there. How about that, from week to week? It is an adventure . . .

We have trod that path before, far too often.

The only original thing to do I guess would be to have the Americans first of all colonise, and then let George Washington III, or somebody, lose it.

Does anybody have any other interesting propositions?

There was one that has not been resolved yet, that there is a possibility, that there is a point in our system where something could be lurking. There's this bit, the other side of the sun, and there could be something there, watching . . .

But, are we being watched? Is there something up there? Is it infectious? Is there something nasty coming in?

A great big eyeball in the sky. Is it edible, or is it watching us or can we colonise it? A lot of problems, each week, they go up to eat it, colonise it or bring it down.

Or they can colonise it and eat it.

And have an eyeglass company sponsor it. There's a lot of possibilities.

This is Hollywood wrapped up in a great big bundle of 'Mad', they want to have a plot which has nothing to do with science fiction, first, then add the science afterwards. This is why all Hollywood science fiction is rotten, rotten to the core because in science fiction many will tell you that plot is hero. And they will never recognise that. Television or films, I am knocking them both. They really will not face the fact. They really should get someone involved in running science fiction who knows something about science fiction. This is a very unusual idea, which they haven't come to yet. There's nobody in that project room who knows anything about science fiction.

Well, I don't know exactly what you mean by 'knows something about science fiction'. What they know on the show and what I know is how to craft a twelve minute act, that ends with you wanting to sit through the commercials wanting to see the next bit of action. This is where we come in. First you have to have an action line, you have to have a James Bond punch-line in each act. I am telling you what the format is or it does not get on the air.

You want a set of characters that people can get to know and they have got to do something every week. So you get 'Star Trek' and they just travel every week in a nice shirt-sleeve environment. They can teleport themselves down onto a new planet, and you can breathe air and there are lots of them and things happen. There is a new set of people. They look, they are all sort of vaguely humanoid and they are all man-like, they are all about five foot six, and they sort of do things.

They change their colours and that is basically it?

You will save production wise. You have your three playable characters and they go off, and you have this whole set of renewable extras every week that do something. This is the kind of thing that you start with. And when you go into big films like 'Star Wars' or 'Close Encounters', again, you get really crappy stories, with terrific lack of moral fibre in them somewhere, so the whole thing collapses in heaps because you are into a great big mass of expensive technology, because you have to try to make one killing. You have 90 minutes and you want to get a billion dollars out of it. The ideas of science fiction, in science fiction books, they cannot be afforded on television or on movies. So somehow the visual side never gets handled properly.

Are you telling me that the constraints are so great that you can not really do science fiction on TV?

Having dealt with filming, I have done TV shows, I have done films in Hollywood, the simple thing is that they think in a simple manner. They feel an experienced screen-writer can write a mystery — and he can; can write a Western, and he can; can write a love story and he can; can write science fiction — and he can't. It happens to be a very narrow specialised field of specialised endeavour and they turn out the same piece of crap, over and over, and wonder why it does not sell. Usually you have a kind of Walter Pidgeon walking around, he's not talking, he's saying 'What the hell am I doing in these funny clothes?' It is a specialised field. People say, you have heard it yourself — I have always wanted to be a writer, I want to be a science fiction writer. My answer always is, you know, I have always wanted to be a brain surgeon, and could I start on you?

This thing is going to bomb and they will never understand why. No one wants to watch the goddam thing. It's a collection of crap, put together, second-hand and this is what kills me. I mean, people now are dealing out of Roddenberry's 'Star Trek'. They are three steps away from the original.

When you do decent science fiction in the films, it makes money. 'Star Wars' made a lot of money. 'Alien' made a lot of money. And they made it because they really were science fiction, and the science fiction fans out there really do know the difference. And they know that 'My Friend the Martian', and this kind of thing, is really hokey and fake, and it is not going to get the ratings.

Well, is there a difference between science fiction and just good plain adventure? OK, then 'Star Wars' is an adventure that happens to take place in a distant galaxy far, far away.

I'll defend 'Star Wars' in that 'Star Wars' put on a dozen or two dozen old science fiction cliches at a great expense and they are fun to look at. It's boys' science fiction, but it's still science fiction. Things happen, the robots don't talk English, they go beepbobobbeeb, you know, it has grand effects and it's big, the concept is big. A little ship goes over and you realise it is as big as the moon, another comes, bigger than that. Oh wow, this is mind blasting. It's not very important, it's just nice, fun to watch. I mean, I much prefer that to a really negative, destructive picture like 'Close Encounters', which is just pure madness. This is anti-science of the worst kind. Everybody, the public thinks that science is made up of flashing lights and strange sounds, and that's all at the end of it. You flash lights and strange sounds, it's anti-science. It's really frightening, that is. It's a cargo-cult. They built these planes out of bamboo so that the Americans would come back. 'Close Encounters' is a cargo cult for the intellectual. We can't do it in earth ways, we're so stupid, we're morons, it's so hard to work politically, we're going to go out there and flash lights and sounds and these guys are going to come down and save mankind. Which is absolutely anti-science. It's a destructive picture.

Is it fair to say that the thrust of science fiction, the purpose of it, is know yourself?

Yes. One of the things it does is shake the admonitory finger at us. In the States, no one wants to read about

Paradise any more. Anti-Paradise, that's great. What science fiction does far too often, and rather boringly at times, is say 'You know, if you don't watch the cockroach will take over. Here's a world full of cockroaches. A cockroach world . . .' You stamp a cockroach like THAT, every time you see one. It's the admonitory finger.

Where does your Buck Rogers get the technology from? Or where do you get the technology to shape his world, the 2500 world?

That's a very good question, because there is no basis in fact for that world.

If you don't go too far ahead, you get into something that's really quite hard to do and that is to take things that are jolly nearly possible and things that will be continued with, the science that we've got now, going forward, and just isolate some of those and then do this admonitory thing and say, look this is the way it's going to go if we do this. So we can use science fiction to live through some of the possibilities of what we have now.

People like to be slightly frightened. If they're too frightened, it's not going to work, they are not going to watch, they will split off. They do not like to be scared out of their minds. It seems you have to get into what people are frightened about now. Do not frighten them too much. Just scratch it and it does not seem to matter very much what the format is providing you look for the things within the technology and where civilisation is frightening them.

Do just what he said. If you can find secret fears, touch those, everyone's going to watch.

There are fears, fears of the destruction of the human race, fear of pollution, and all these things. Get into some real fears. Take a fear for each sequence, now, what if . . . the cockroaches take over?

8   COMPUTERS IN AMERICAN MOVIES: THE FEARS, THE DREAMS, THE REALITY

Suzanne Landa

*Formerly with the RAND Corporation, Suzanne Landa is best
known for her studies of the use of computer technology in the
movie industry. Her contribution was originally a run through of
scenes from movies with a science fiction element which contained
robots, androids, and computers, and was accompanied by slides
and film extracts. This has meant substantial editing. What is left
however is still probably the best catalogue of computing technology
as portrayed in the American movies, certainly the funniest and
wittiest.*

I feel that entertainment is truly the last earthly frontier for
automation and that the next decade will see some exciting
results of the union of computers and automation.

But what is the situation like today? A number of the
movies I am going to discuss are based on novels. I do not
want to get into a discussion about who should be credited
— or discredited — for what you are seeing on the screen:
whether it is the novelist, the screen writer or the special
effects person. I do not also intend to discuss the actual
source of each machine's physical manifestation on the
screen.

Sometimes the hardware is built from scratch as was the
case for the movie 'Adesset'. The movie featured a computer
called 'The Electro-Magnetic Memory And Research Arith-
metic Calculator', or EMMARAC for short. Designed by
special effects man Ray Kellard, EMMARAC consisted of
nine thousand light bulbs, ten miles of wire and several

dozen switches, dimmers, faders and special transformers.

Sometimes hardware is borrowed from computer companies, as in 'The Forbin Project', CDC provided over five million dollars worth of computer equipment and supplies. It took an entire sound stage to house the equipment and the CDC consultants to make it all work.

A third source of computer equipment is the computer facilities at the studios. Both MGM and Universal Studios have computer facilities, and in Universal's case you can see it in many television shows, for instance *Quincy*.

Over at Disney, we have two Univac 90/80s and one 90/70. And, at Fox, until recently the computer programmers were housed in the basement, an annexe. Somehow the computer was mysteriously elevated in the eyes of management and was moved upstairs into beautiful, new surroundings. And I'm sure we will soon see a Fox release featuring their system.

Software has become a major prop in these stories, especially computer graphics. Gary Martins, now at the Rand Corporation, provided the first computer graphics playing the part of computer graphics. In the 1964 Warner Brothers' film, 'Brainstorm', the script called for Jeffrey Hunter to go up to the computer, pull out a card, register a look of shock and amazement, put the card back in the computer and walk away. Well, Gary argued convincingly that a more accurate and dramatic interaction between Hunter and the computer would be through computer graphics. Now, computer graphics did not become an overnight star. In fact, four years later, in the movie '2001', the control visuals were in fact animations masquerading as computer graphics. Actually computer graphics cast as computer graphics did not catch the public's fancy until 'Star Wars'. Today, of course, hardware and such software as graphics are commonly seen even on television.

Now, if you ask somebody on the street 'What do you think of when I say computers in the movies?', the most likely response you get is 'robots'. To be sure this is a recent association with computer technologies, but one I do not think we should ignore. So let us take a quick look at what I call the Top Ten movie star robots of film. We have to start with the 1926 silent film 'Metropolis', which featured the first cinema robot. The first movie star robot was female. But Maria was also evil and eventually burned, or rather melted, at the stake. The most famous cinema robot was the best loved metal man of all, the Tin Man from 'The Wizard of Oz'. In 'The Day the Earth Stood Still', the robot Gort with his master aimed to preserve peace on earth, but the US Army would have none of it. TOBOR, which is robot spelled backwards, loved his inventor; while this love destroyed him, he managed to destroy a few people along the way. And in 'Forbidden Planet', Robbie the Robot cooks, cleans and renders weapons inoperable. But, to Anne Francis' dismay, he still wets on the carpet. Now, at a loss as to how to make the cinema robot more anthropomorphic, Hollywood brought us our first animal robot, Mechanicon. Well, the public was not impressed, so Hollywood went back to the drawing board and came up with yet another robot man or rather child. 'Silent Running' featured the youthful exploits of the miniature robots, Hughie, Dewie and Louie. In 'Logan's Run' we return to the evil, mechanical man, but in yet another form. Box is half man, half robot. And 'Star Wars', of course, brought us robotic comedy. R2 D2 and C3 PO captured, in a mechanical way of course, the humour of our favourite film funny men, Laurel and Hardy. Which brings us up to the most recent screen robot. Over 50 years after Maria in 'Metropolis', we have TWEEKY in 'Buck Rogers'. Of these ten robots, seven are portrayed as good. You will see in the next few minutes that computers have not fared quite so well in the movies.

But before we leave robots, let's take a quick look at androids in the movies. Woody Allen's 'Sleeper' is set in the 22nd century, where society is totally regulated and staffed with android butlers. In 'West World', androids are programmed to cater to the whims of people visiting an adult Disneyland. In one scene, an android, and I quote, '. . . is having a new mini-computer installed'! And in 'Future World', the androids of 'West World' return to the screen, but with far more advanced capabilities. Clark the Dummy can play poker — and design nuclear power plants!

And now to the subject of *computers* in the movies. At the National Computer Conference in 1979 John Oakland of IBM, in making the key-note address, commented on the anthropomorphic view of computers and how it has resulted in . . . paranoia. Well the movies, in reflecting this, have seemed to reinforce it. But where do we begin? You will find the subject of computers included in the 1960 Film Index, listed notably between composers and con-men. But I think we should begin this discussion a little bit earlier with the 1955 film '1984'. In this movie, society is controlled by Big Brother. In one scene people were seated at terminals, searching through what we now call data-bases of information on other people. This is an incredibly accurate prediction of a partitioned office of today.

In 'The Invisible Boy', an evil supercomputer plots to control the world. No one suspects, of course, that the computer is the master of its own plans; rather the plot is blamed on the Russians.

'Death's Set' was the first movie to deal with computers in the here-and-now. Spencer Tracy plays an engineer with responsibility for installing a computer in Katherine Hepburn's office. In one scene, Hepburn is probably being accused of making an unauthorised software modification! In 'The

Honeymoon Machine', Steve McQueen uses a battleship's computer to win at roulette. He signals table information back to the computer, which is fed in and winning numbers are then calculated and flashed back to McQueen on shore. Unfortunately, Russian and US officials intercept these signals and interpret them as aggressive, military instructions. McQueen is in trouble and the computer is no help. And, in 'Doctor Strangelove', a bomber-base commander orders an attack on Russia, because he believes the Communists are sapping the strength of America through water fluoridation. While the theatre audience is given the impression at one point that the Group Captain played by Peter Sellers is calling the President, we all know that that's simply an euphemism for the programmer!

In 'Alphaville', Alphaville is the capital of our galaxy in 1984, and it is ruled by a giant computer, Alpha 60. Earth sends a super secret agent to destroy the computer because it is logically executing all inhabitants who show signs of love and conscience. The working title of this movie was 'Trazan versus IBM'. In 1967, we have 'Billion Dollar Brain'. In this movie Michael Caine is involved in planning an attack on Russia with the aid of, what else, a billion dollar computer. Karl Maddern seems to be saying to Caine at one point that the billion dollars is only for hardware, software is extra.

1968 was a good year for computers in the movies. We had 'Hot Millions', in which Peter Ustinov plays an embezzler whose crime is discovered by a computer. After he is released from prison, he decides to continue his life of crime by becoming a computer expert. And, of course, in 1968, we had '2001', featuring HAL, a computer with a dominating personality — and problems. HAL is portrayed as more human than the humans in the movie. We also had 'Barbarella'. I bet you do not even remember that there was a computer in this movie. Well, 'Barbarella' is memorable for more reasons than the obvious. This movie predicted a new development in our industry. In one scene, according to the production notes, Barbarella is consulting with her personal computer which provides her with weather reports, awakens her daily and acts as a companion on her long intergalactic flights. And we might do well to note Barbarella's unique but successful method for interacting with her personal computer which is to talk to it on her knees. Then there was 'The Forbin Project' which featured the US Defence's computer Colossus and the Russian equivalent Guardian (I should say near-equivalent because it was really a very patriotic film!). I read the final script for this and it is interesting to note what was cut out. The astonishment of the Russians at the speed at which the computers communicate was still included, but the fact that that communication speed was a thousand words per minute had been dropped. For those of you who missed the film, I think one of the most interesting things is that we find out in this movie what happens to computer analysts who overload the system. Colossus had them executed.

1970 brought up 'The Computer Wore Tennis Shoes'. In this Disney movie, Kurt Russel plays a college student who accidentally gets all the computer's memory transferred into his flunking brain. You might find the Press Release for this more entertaining than the movie — and I quote — 'Credibility has always been a rule of thumb for any and all of Walt Disney's pictures, regardless of how far out the theme may be. In this movie the realm of credibility becomes a tricky one to master, since the story deals with a computer'.

In 1970 we also have a Swedish entry into the genre, 'The Gladiators', a precursor to 'Rollerball'. In this movie, massive computer war games, called peace games, are sponsored by a spaghetti company. The Swedes, you see, had discovered that the live/die alternative, being basically binary, could be left up to a computer. And we also learn in 'The

Gladiators' what to do during a computer mal-function, or at least what the Swedes do, and what else would that be but make love. Unfortunately, once the computer is reactivated and working, the new lovers are discovered and executed. In 1970 too we have my favourite computer flick of all times, 'The Sphinx' spelt just as you see here, which may partially explain why it only played one week. The story will explain the rest. The Sphinx features a computer called, and I'll let you figure out the acronym, the Mechanical Oracle That Helps Americans. In this movie the US Secret Service consults a computer about the kidnapping of a number of American show biz people by Communist Albania. (All these stories I'm telling you are true, I don't make them up!). The computer responds with a plan to form a rock group to tour Albania and find the prisoners. And in it you can see, according to the computer plan, a member of the rock group maintaining his cover by autographing Albanian bottoms. Now, the plan is temporarily foiled when it is discovered that the map to the hideout is tattooed on the bellies of three women, in London, Rome and Copenhagen. But finally the hideout, a castle, is found and the computer directs the group to stage a rock concert nearby and the loud vibrations from the concert crumble the walls of the castle, freeing the American show biz people. Warner Brothers was shocked that I tracked that one down. In 'The Thief Who Came to Dinner', Ryan O'Neill plays a computer analyst whose work with computers has turned him into a very boring fellow. His wife leaves him and his computers and not even a very pretty new lady in his life can shake him out of his digital dullness. In 'The Terminal Man', a computer scientist suffering from a mental disorder has a 'mini-computer' implanted in his brain to control these seizures. In 'The Manitu', another one of my favourites, a lump on Susan Strassberg's neck is diagnosed as the foetus of a 400-year old, reincarnated, medicine man.

Eventually he is reborn, full-grown but a monster devil. To destroy him Tony Curtis, Susan's boyfriend brings a modern-day medicine-man to the hospital to use his manitu, or his spirit against the old man's manitu. Since they are both Indian spirits, the plan fails but all things, not just people, have manitus or spirits and Curtis, suddenly enlightened, explains to Singing Rock, the old man's going to be in trouble. But Singing Rock persuades Curtis to try to take a more spiritual rather than physical approach by calling on the manitu of the hospital's computer. And so we see Curtis and Singing Rock chanting, 'Manitu of machine, take my love, take my faith, oh machine manitu, kill.'. And the computer's manitu dutifully zaps the old man.

In the recent release of 'Buck Rogers', society in the twenty-fifth century is governed by a commerce of computers. According to Leslie Stevens, one of the writers of Buck, the idea isn't that far-fetched. Stevens says, 'If you pump in a sufficient amount of wise, intelligent, logical information, you will have a wise, intelligent, logical computer'.

I have some observations on this movie's portrayal of future computers. Novelists, film-makers and even our own technologists have viewed the future as being controlled by a mammoth base of computers. As we have feared this, we have dreamed of the ultimate computer as being an intelligent, controllable robotic cast in the figure of man or woman. Recently artificial intelligence experts tell us that neither the dream nor the fear are likely to become a reality. Rather the future automated society will employ little boxes of intelligence which can be carried around. The Buck Rogers' computers called QUADs capture cinematically this concept. They are the small round containers. Immobile themselves, people, and robots like Tweeky, must carry them about. Now, I don't want to spoil 'Alien' for any of you but for computer buffs the movie is really a comedy. The opening sequence takes place on board a space tug set in the far distant future. The camera zooms in on texts being displayed on a CRT to the sounds of a teletype! Better yet is the padded cell approach to the computer control room. But the nine thousand recycled lights from Death Set could drive anyone crazy. The movie also features a scientist who, when the computer cannot decode an encrypted message, studiously reviews the strings of zeros and ones at the terminal. Of course, they did not explain that she spent fifty years as a systems engineer.

And now to my favourite sub-category of computers in the movies, that is computers and sex in the movies, where computers truly become anthropomorphic. My husband asserts, no, no, prays that I am the only person in the world who finds a picture of a computer erotic.

I will look at the same areas: robots, androids and then computers in the movies. We will start with 'Flesh Gordon' where Flesh and Dale Artur fall down a toilet and end up in the evil Emperor Wang's palace. Wang turns three rapist robots loose on them but Flesh manages to, and I do quote, 'blow their circuits'. This movie was nominated for an Academy Award, for special effects. But right before the nominees were announced publicly, the category was quietly dropped that year, and 'The Poseidon Adventure' received a special technical award. In 'Doctor G and The Bikini Machine', Vincent Price plays a mathematician who builds an extraordinary computer. After flashing lights and spewing forth fluid, the computer outputs beautiful, female androids. Under Price's direction, they seduce men of influence so that he can control the world. In the X-rated film, 'How to Make a Doll' (I want to reiterate, I'm not making these stories up) Doctors Percy and West also build a computer that creates beautiful female androids. Dr. West unfortunately dies of heart failure during an orgy with these creations. But, his brain lives on in the computers so he can continue to vicariously get pleasure observing Percy's exploits. Well, Percy tires of it all and wants to get out of this and he plots to erase West's memory. But West discovers the plan and creates a horde of beauties to amorously placate Percy. But Percy has really had enough, he destroys the androids by tearing up their punched cards!

And, we have 'The Stepford Wives', in which all the husbands in a suburban community instigate a perfidious plan to totally dominate their wives. Each wife is turned into a perfectly subservient, home-maker robot providing sex on cue. Just as an aside, I thought you might like to hear one of the suggestions Columbia offered local communities on how to promote this film, and that is to run a Perfect Wife contest, in which husbands would write in, 'My wife is the perfect wife because . . .'

Another X-rated computer film was 'The Love Clinic', featuring a computer that gives lessons in sexual fulfilments to a young lady. She in return pledges her fidelity to the computer, a fact that enrages her husband. I think the interesting thing about this movie is the casting of the computer: not as a pretty or handsome face but as a noble character.

And yet another X-rated film was 'The Curious Female', set in the twenty-second century where a master computer rules a society devoid of love and romance. But a group of friends get together and decide to break the law and view a 1969 release entitled 'The Three Virgins'. The old film shows the sexual awakening of the women through a computer dating service called Cupid. Unfortunately the group is discovered and arrested. But in the closing scene we see the master computer re-running the film for its own enlightenment.

'THX 1138' covers a lot of categories, yet it is really another version of the premise that all passions will be forbidden in centuries to come. Our stars have dropped a drug which is used to control the populace and they begin to experience emotions for the first time. And they are caught in the forbidden act of love-making and subsequently tried by computer.

In 'Everything You Wanted To Know About Sex, But Were Afraid to Ask', Woody Allen plays a frightened sperm on Red-Alert under the control of the brain which is portrayed as a mad-house of computers, and Tony Randall plays the part of the Emission Control computer. And, of course we had 'Demonseed', a simple tale of computer meets girls, computer gets girl and computer begets god-knows-what. Julie Christie's husband has devised a computer called Proteus which suffers strange, male-like urges. At one point a mobile unit under the control of Proteus grabs Julie for the big, or more likely bad, moment. This is followed by a scene with bed-posts and flying sparks, which must be Hollywood's idea of electronic . . . well, I'll let you fill that in. And the resulting progeny of Julie and Proteus terrifies the 'family's' computer analyst, who discovers that his scientific expertise is no help against a monster born of woman and computer.

There really are a lot of other movies I have had to leave out: such porno flicks as 'Nine Ages of Nakedness', and 'How to Seduce A Playboy'; all of these deal with computers. Then there is 'Our Man Flint', 'Jigsaw' and other movies like that. But essentially the survey is complete.

Now why does all this happen? What I have discovered is that there is a lot of translation that goes on at each stage of the production of a movie. You can make a script technially accurate, but then the producer and the director have their hand in it, and the special effects men have their hand in it and unless you keep an eye all along the way, you are still going to get some of these strange interpretations. And also the stories simply reflect feelings of the populace. They are making movies about what they think people feel. And so, unless our attitudes, our paranoias change, I do not see immediate change in sight.

Let me recapitulate. Science fiction writers, film makers, and even technologists have forecast future society as being controlled by mammoth banks of computers. Sci-Fi movies that support this theme are 'The Forbin Project', '2001', 'Alphaville', and 'The Invisible Boy'. While the public has feared this, we have dreamed of ultimate computers as intelligent controllable robots cast in the figure of man or woman: Robby in 'Forbidden Planet', R2D2 and C3PO in 'Star Wars', Huey, Dewey and Louey in 'Silent Running', and the plastic robot butlers in 'Sleeper'.

But now artificial intelligence experts tell us that neither the fear nor the dream is likely to become reality. Rather, computers in tomorrow's society will be small boxes of intelligence that we carry around and connect to perform various functions. This concept is partially introduced in 'Buck Rogers', with the small round container-like computers called Quads.

In addition to the change in size and appearance of future computers in sci-fi movies, there has also been a shift away from the malevolent all powerful machines to computers as everyday tools. That is, computers are beginning to be portrayed as people amplifiers. We saw this in 'Star Wars' and in 'Battlestar Galactica'. This shift should not be surprising in that it parallels our adjustment to major technological change. If the shift continues, it means a move towards that class of science fiction called speculative fiction. This places more emphasis on human behaviour and social evolution than on technological change. An example of this genre to be found on American television is 'The Lathe of Heaven'. I think speculative fiction will produce far more fascinating films than 'science' fiction.

PART FOUR
Introduction

We return from the wilder reaches of some science fiction related activity to science fact, and the return has been made as gentle as possible. It is bridged by Arthur C. Clarke.

Now no attempt to try to connect science fiction and science fact would be complete without the intervention of Arthur Clarke. His intervention is even more necessary when the meeting is in part to consider the creation and impact of future devices on society and culture, for this is the main field of his work.

Today, he is known both as the doyen of science fiction writers (though that perhaps could be disputed by Isaac Asimov: a story well known in science fiction circles has it that they address each other as the world's second best science fiction writer) and as the science fiction writer whose real claim to fame rests uniquely on a science fact paper, that famous first essay which postulates the likelihood of a communications satellite network, and gives the orbits that would be required. He can truthfully claim to be the father of the telecommunications satellite.

Arthur C. Clarke seems to receive an invitation to lecture from some one or some body almost every other day, invitations which he generally turns down. So I went out to Colombo in Sri Lanka to see him, to interview him in his house and garden surrounded by the songs of birds and the street cries of hawkers. What follows was eventually presented as an audio visual 'entertainment' using music, quotations from a television lecture he gave in the USA, and from the film he scripted, the Stanley Kubrik produced and directed award-winning epic '2001, A Space Odyssey'. Only the sounds and pictures have been deleted.

It may be hard to credit it, but the Clarke paper on the telecommunications satellites was written over thirty years ago. What has happened since, what is happening now, are both well and neatly caught by Pearce Wright, the Science Editor of *The Times* in the piece that follows.

Like Clarke, he shows how critical improved communications are to change, and gives some of the flavour of that change. Both writers assume, though unstated, and perhaps almost by instinct, that the world's intercommunications satellite system is going to continue to grow under a sort of Anglo Saxon umbrella.

Let them however, as much as is possible, speak for themselves.

9 INTERVIEW WITH ARTHUR C. CLARKE

Rex Malik

Wednesday 25th July 1979

R.M. Arthur C. Clarke lives in Sri Lanka: the land of serendip, of happenstance. And happenstance plays a part in the genesis of his latest, and he claims his last, book, The Fountains of Paradise. *In it he suggests that it is possible to connect a synchronous orbit satellite and earth by means of an umbilical cord, a space elevator. That will do away with the need for space shots as we know them, and space shuttles.* The Fountains of Paradise *is also set in Sri Lanka: poetic licence as the equator passes to the south. Five hundred years ago, however, that would not have helped him; he would still have been burned at the stake for trying to connect Heaven and Earth. But, can he see a 40,000 kilometre long space elevator actually being built, and near Sri Lanka at that?*

A.C. I exagerrated that. The necessity of a high altitude site too is probably greatly exaggerated: poetic licence. It would be more suitable here than anywhere else. I think that when it is anchored almost anywhere around the equator it will probably be suitable enough, but this is something that people have been doing some very high-powered mathematics about. I certainly couldn't give a definitive answer. It does, however, fascinate me that I should have settled down in the one spot in the world, many years ago, which is nearest to the most stable spot in the gravitational geoid: pure coincidence.

R.M.   It is then a serious possibility of the near future?

A.C.   Oh yes. I am taking it very seriously, as are more and more people. There is a rapidly expanding literature on the subject and there is a feeling getting around that this may be possible in about one hundred years' time because if you extrapolate the increase in the strength of materials it does seem a feasibility some time in the next century. There are the materials theoretically which can do this. So fabulously expensive that they have only been made in small quantities. The first Uranium 235 after all was not visible to the naked eye.

R.M.   At this point I said, 'You are going to get into trouble with the world ecologists, for now you want to tinker with the structure of the planet.'

A.C.   Oh, We are not doing very much to the planet. It's negligible compared to the mass of the planet. The first space elevator might weigh a few million tons, but that is not very much compared with things we do on the earth's surface.

R.M.   But, Arthur Clarke is not just interested in space. His interests, his puzzlements are also more earth bound. Science fiction in his case often begins with science theory or the search for it.

A.C.   I haven't heard the details yet. Somebody's sending signals now through hundred of miles of solid earth via a burst of nutrinos. Theoretically impossible, but you know the nutrino makes the earth as transparent as glass, in fact much more transparent than glass because it will go through light years of solid lead without any noticeable inconvenience. We've noticed a situation where there are now more fundamental particles than there are elements. One feels there is something wrong somewhere! Is there another hierarchy above or below this? Will there be more and more for ever and ever? Or will we finally reach the end of the line somewhere? I just don't know.

R.M.   And, here is another puzzle, an old puzzle, which almost all science fiction writers and science fiction buffs would wish were solved.

A.C.   It is only in more recent years that the idea that there might be valid physics beyond the speed of light has come into the picture. No one has found the slightest evidence for it but there are such fantastic things popping up in physics now that no one will be particularly surprised if it does turn out to be the case. The question is whether the domain of super light velocity will ever be accessible in any way, or will it be such a separate universe that it wouldn't exist really as far as we are concerned?

R.M.   Let us leave the realm of currently insoluble puzzles and change the pace. Let's ask about science fiction of the last quarter of a century. Does it change the role of science fiction writers? Does it change the practice of writing science fiction?

A.C.   I think science fiction is so complex that almost anything you say about science fiction is true nowadays. Obviously there is a profound difference now because there is a very much wider basis on which we can write our science fiction. But let me stress the point that science fiction is not usually predictive anyway: it is extrapolative. It says 'What if?', not 'There will be so-and-so'. In fact, much of science fiction is anti-predictive; 'I don't try to predict the future, I try to prevent it'. And that is one of the most important roles of science fiction; to stop some futures happening. Of course, many science fiction writers now are virtually scientists, so that is another change from the past. Though quite a number of scientists in previous periods did write science fiction, usually under assumed names, now a lot of them do it under their own names.

R.M. That does not mean that the scientists or science fiction writers will necessarily spot in time what should be obvious.

A.C. You know, science fiction almost completely failed to predict the advent of the personal computer. Although Isaac Asimov does have an accurate description of one in one of his early 'Foundation' stories, nobody dreamed that within a few years slide-rules and mathematical tables were going to be obsolete. This is the most incredible technological revolution of all time. I think that what we are doing now, in a sense, is creating our own successors. We have seen the first crude beginnings of artificial intelligence, though it does not really exist yet at any level because our most complex computers are still morons, high-speed morons but still morons. Nevertheless, some of them are capable of learning, and we will one day be able to design systems that can go on improving themselves. At that stage we will have the possibility of machines that can outpace their creators and therefore become more intelligent than us.

HAL from '2001' I am sorry Dave . . . I am afraid that this mission is too important to allow me to let you jeopardise it.

R.M. That was the voice of HAL from '2001'. Let us not misunderstand what Arthur Clarke expects in the future, but let HAL tell it.

HAL The 9000 Series is the most reliable computer ever made. No 9000 computer has ever made a mistake or distorted information. We are all, by any practical definition of the words, fool-proof and incapable of error. My mission responsibilities range over the entire operation of the ship so I am constantly occupied. I am putting myself to the fullest possible use which is all I think that any conscious entity can ever hope to do.

R.M. *But HAL is but one step forward, there are others. Among them there is a growing link of the planet by communication satellite. But should we bother? Is it necessary? In these energy conscious days Arthur Clarke would reply, Yes. And as he says, the effects could be major.*

A.C. I think to a large extent, it would make a big impact on the transportation industry. I mean I see very little point in transportation for business. Transportation for pleasure is always increasing but not very much for business I am sure.

R.M. *As you would expect from the father of the communications satellite, he has thought about how satellites might be used for many years. There was 'I Remember Babylon', in which direct television broadcasting was used to purvey pornography. But, would the machines allow it? It is not an odd question, in* Dial F for Frankenstein. *But let Arthur tell it.*

A.C. It is based in the near future, when they are just putting in the last link in the global television satellite system, and at that point the system passes the threshold, the critical point, and becomes a self-conscious entity. And that is the end of the human race.

R.M. *Which begs a question, how would the network talk to us? We don't have to wait for Frankenstein, there is a problem, a serious problem, and it is one of language.*

A.C.   For a long time I have been registering the impact on language. I have said many times that if we did have a global TV system which was dominated by one language, that would become the language of all mankind. I think it is going to happen. It won't be the only language of all mankind but it means that we will all share a common language. It will probably be in English. It will lead to a quantum jump in understanding in many ways. Although you can't be sure, because, after all, we and the Irish speak more or less the same language and we do have some problems. Do you have a problem?

R.M.   Yes. I do have a problem. Won't we need a universal translator within this communications network? That is where he begins. That is not where he ends.

A.C.   I don't know about a universal translator, that is going to be a terribly difficult problem, isn't it? Translating from one language to another. Although, they now have little pocket computer dictionaries. You press the button and get a translation into the other language. This appears on the screen and you just show the picture to the natives of the land. Whether we can bypass language, whether that is possible, I just don't know. Whether all human minds have enough in common so we might be able to communicate without using language.

R.M.   Which leads to an interesting possibility. If we cannot build a translation capability into the network system can perhaps build it into people?

A.C.   They will build it into our brains. We will have modules that just plug in and plug out . . .

R.M.   Yes, instead of talking about heart transplants we will be talking about brain transplants.

A.C.   Brain Transplants. If you want to go for a holiday in a foreign country, you just plug in that language. I am not sure how seriously I take this idea, but, considering what we have seen happening in the past, I'd hate to rule it out completely.

R.M.   *But what if the intelligence fails? What happens if the most incredible technology of all time lets you down? In* Into The Comet *the crew of his space vehicle find just that.*

A.C.   When the computer breaks down, they have masses of calculations to do to come home. There is a Japanese crew member and he just sets to. They build abacusses for each member of the crew and he programs the crew with their abacusses, a giant computer, you see . . .

R.M.   *All this from Sri Lanka, which is perhaps as good a place from which to survey the race inventing its own future, however you think that is likely to work out.*

A.C.   Well, I am fairly optimistic about Sri Lanka because I think they have got the population explosion under control, the birth rate has been falling off quite rapidly. The country has plenty of natural resources except oil, but possibly sunlight can make up for that, though, not in the near future. And, even if the crunch comes, and world civilisation collapses, this place has a little chance of survival. Perhaps Sri Lanka and New Zealand?

R.M.   *But Arthur Clarke does not really have a firm view of an end either of technology or us. He would say that this is not really his function. However, towards the end of our conversation (he is gadget mad and he was showing me his video-player) he did say this.*

A.C.   This is how the race is going to end. We are all going to sit glued to our TV games and civilisation will collapse.

Maybe Eliot had it right.

HAL in '2001' Stop Dave. I'm afraid. I'm Afraid Dave. Dave. My mind is going. I can feel it.

10 PROFITS – AND PROPHETS – OF SPACE

Pearce Wright

*Pearce Wright has been covering space activities since the early days
in the fifties. He holds a degree in electronic engineering. He has
been first Science Correspondent and then Science Editor of* The
Times *for the last fifteen years.*

The title you have in front of you is *Profits and Prophets of
Space*. I have thought about it and decided that a different
title would be better. It says that

> The only difference between men and boys,
> Is that men like to play with larger toys.

And it struck me that that is what a lot of science fiction is
about.

To launch into this subject let me quote another line from
A Midsummer Night's Dream, which is:

> 'I'll put a girdle about the earth
> In forty minutes . . .' said Puck.

Now, one of my more usual cribs as a science correspondent
who writes about space is *Rockets, Missiles and Men in
Space*, by Willy Ley, one of the people who worked with
Werner Von Braun in the early days, in Germany. He tells
me that there is a fat chance, of course, of putting a girdle
around the earth in forty minutes, because that's an imposs-
ibly short period of time in which to encircle the earth with

anything that would not burn up. So my idea of suggesting that Shakespeare was also a science fiction writer was upstaged.

Journeys into space have given rise to a wealth of fiction, reaching deep into antiquity. What is probably the first work of fiction, describing what we now call space travel, was the *Vera Historia* (True History) of Lucian of Samosata. He was a Greek sophist and satirist who wrote within half a century of Plutarch. His plot contained all the right ingredients — a trip through space; a landing on another world, a description of that world and the return journey. All done on an elegant sailing vessel which was lifted from the sea by a violent whirlwind and carried to the moon. Lucian's tale stood for centuries. But, in another space fantasy, Orlando Furioso, the hero, travels to the moon in a chariot drawn by four red horses. According to the author, Ludovico Ariosto, the moon had most of the natural features of this planet, with cities and towns and castles, too.

Far more ingenious was David Russen's *Iter Lunare*. He had a giant spring constructed on top of a mountain to catapult a man into space toward the moon! But, it was a couple of centuries from Ariosto's horse-drawn coach to the works that had something resembling modern science fiction.

In 1775, a book by Louis Guillaume had the characteristics associated with contemporary science fiction. It tells of Ormissais, a Mercurian who arrives on earth to tell his story to one, Nadir, an oriental. It seems that the mercurian inventor called Scintilla had created an ingenious, electric flying chariot which he demonstrated to his fellow scientists, despite their scorn and ridicule. Ormisais was so certain that the chariot would not work that he, flippantly, agreed to fly it and, to his surprise, he was carried through space. After the fairly standard forms of adventure, he crashes on earth and relates his story. It indicated the change of fiction into science fiction, because readers were beginning to be sufficiently aware of science to expect more realism in their fiction. However this connection with reality was limited to the means of travel. The wildest details about the nature of the planets and their imaginary inhabitants were still acceptable and, to a large extent, still are.

The toys still dominate with robots, artificial intelligence machines, laser weapons, electro-magnetically operated transporters of people and so on.

Now, if you haven't met the 'Toy Theory of Western History' before, the originator — as far as I know — is a marvellous man called Koenig, the Director of Development at the Institute for Scientific Information in Philadelphia. His thesis is that the excess of militarism which has plagued Western society for the last century and a half rests on motives which society consistently under-estimates. Put simply, it is a desire to 'play with toys'. In this context the phrase means — manipulating devices ·which are both novel and high-performance, and devices which 'push the State of the Art.'

Since playing with toys is not perceived as a mature, man-like thing to do, a fascinating explanation is offered by Koenig of how most of society manages not to recognise this unpalatable state of affairs in a subconscious rejection.

He asks, 'How many people are, on the face of it, willing to spend a vast amount of their national resource on a Toy Cooperative?' The answer would be very few. So, the militarists and technophiles — the fashionable description of the famous military industrial alliance — rationalise their 'Toy Coop' into the familiar form: 'National Defense', 'National Preparedness', the 'Missile Gap' and so on. According to Koenig, this rationalisation has been determined in large part by the nature of the technology itself. The most enjoyable toys are the most powerful, those that push the State of the Art hardest.

At last perhaps you can see the gleam of a spacecraft around the corner, but, just before we get there, I wanted to add that, certainly for 50 years, perhaps 100, the nature of technology itself has been such that those applications which push the State of the Art hardest have been defensible only for the military. A P40 at supersonic speeds is much more exciting than a DC-3. A missile cruiser pushing its 4,000 tons with 100,000 horsepower offers a pleasure far more visceral than a merchantman using a quarter of that power to push ten times that weight. The cruiser's power-to-weight ratio is obviously greater by more than an order of magnitude.

Even in the West, the military machine can scarcely be called democratic. But, in a sense of a populist institution which can make available the toys of our culture to millions of people for whom they would have been otherwise unobtainable, it provides a service.

If I had to defend the 'Toy Thesis', I think I should pick space technology as the particular case in which to argue the generality. You will notice in sketching out the early trends in the written word on space travel I avoided mentioning that not all the works were speculative fiction, even before Newton. By the time Jules Verne was ready to fire his immense gun, *From the Earth to the Moon*, there was an enthusiastic readership for science fiction. By the turn of the century, three very important people acknowledged they had been inspired by Verne; Tsiolkowsky in Russia, Oberth in Germany, and Goddard in the States. We are now talking about the three people who were the founders of European Soviet and American rocket technology. Goddard indeed only just missed seeing the first satellites in orbit. We are talking about people who in a sense are really my early contemporaries. The rockets which made space exploration feasible have their direct ancestry in these three men and all their biographies in great detail actually acknowledge, in particular, the work of Jules Verne.

The main period of rivalry between Russia and America after the launch of Sputnik I is fascinating, if only because the forecasts and technical studies about the possibilities of space technology presented to the Armed Services by the high-powered think tanks (assembled in World War Two) turned out to be remarkably accurate. The US Navy takes the credit for being the first American group to formally study the notion of artificial Satellites. The idea was put to the Committee for evaluating the feasibility of rocketry in 1943. Its first action was to place a contract with the California Institute of Technology to investigate the relationships between carrier vehicle performance, the weight of a satellite and the height of its orbit. A subsequent proposal was for a launcher fuelled by liquid oxygen and liquid hydrogen with a thrust of 100,000 pounds. The empty rocket casing would be left in orbit to become the satellite. All this took place in 1943. More than ten years later we find the same idea being adopted when the Atlas Centaur gave the first communications message from space. That was the one with a pre-recorded magnetic tape on board.

The Army Air Corps in the States, as it was then, went on a different tack with a multi-stage design produced by the Project Rand staff. It was eventually decided that the only way to put an object into space was by a two stage rocket. The Project Rand staff was then a part of Douglas Aircraft. They did their work with the help of Research and Development teams in North American Aviation, Northrop Aviation and many other of the large American companies. The specification they produced covered communications, meteorological and reconnaissance satellites.

This was the first of the many reports to come from Rand

that brought the theory closer to realisation. There was a particularly interesting one that was prefaced by an impassioned political statement. It said, 'Achievement of a satellite craft by the United States would inflame the imagination of mankind, and probably would produce repercussions in the world comparable with the explosion of the Atomic Bomb.' That was more than a decade before the first satellite was built and, of course, proved prophetic when Sputnik I soared into orbit. But, in the late forties, the American Department of Defence would not authorize a satellite venture until some military application was clearly specified: the emphasis remained on war-head carrying missiles.

A group within the US Air Force revised the Rand proposals in 1949. They added to the arguments on communications, reconnaissance and meteorological satellites the rider that, 'Such a development would provide a display of American scientific and technical leadership that would be a powerful, psychological factor in the Cold War'. As we all know, the tables were turned and it was the Russians who demonstrated that the mere presence of an artificial satellite in the sky would have a profound psychological effect on the opponent.

Before the first satellites were launched the Rand reports had been refined into a special project by the Ballistic Missile Division of the United States Air Force into a design specification for a nuclear test monitor in space. The latest version of that type of detector is an enormous telescope. It's an infra-red telescope, an enormous object to be carried into space.

The navigation satellite that is in fact becoming the basis of the American general positioning system throughout the world is the Navstar project. It derives from a proposition to give nuclear submarines a position to within plus or minus

150 metres anywhere on the globe. It was expanded into the civil area for all the obvious reasons that everybody else in Aviation, Maritime work and so on had the same needs, but because of the dominance of military interests in space launchings, the amount of money spent in the first decade of space technology is very difficult to assess, for like all defence and military budgets it is really wrapped up as a global sum. Even in the States, where they account for these things publicly better than anywhere else in the world, it is not broken down.

The issue became more open, of course, with the Apollo project, costing £10,000 million. Although it was a vast sum, in the same decade the war in Vietnam cost ten times as much. Be that as it may, since it is around the tenth anniversary of the Apollo landing on the moon, the question readily comes to mind again of whether or not it was worth it. Or, could the money have been better spent. In practice we all know that resources are seldom allocated for the purposes we individually rate as the most socially, politically or economically desirable. It is fair to assume, therefore, that in the judgement of a large proportion of us, it was well spent and could not have been better spent in some other way. So the question is important only about the guide it gives us to future behaviour.

What has impressed me about Apollo is the lasting awareness that it really has created about Planet Earth. It was displayed as the jewel of the solar system, an oasis in a universal wilderness measured in millions of light years.

But was £10,000 million too high a price to pay for that stirring of human consciousness? I don't believe that unmanned probes landing on the moon would have done it, even if they had gone for one-tenth of the price. Many scientists opposed to the manned landings wanted unmanned scientific craft to go instead. These, they believed, would have given the geologists and physicists more — and better — information about the age, origin and structure of the moon (or at least more exact data than the astronauts managed with their cavortings). It is doubtful however if the impact on the human psyche would have been as great, or as powerful.

For a moment I want to skim across the profits of space, not so much in terms of the return in cash on an investment, but in direct benefits flowing from being able to do the new things, such as observe cloud cover continually on a global basis. The meteorological satellites have yielded a great reward in storm warnings, the planning of irrigation systems and so on. Their successors, the Landsat satellites, have enhanced the techniques of observing the state of the world's crops, finding mineral deposits, identifying diseases in forests and crops, identifying earthquake fault zones, tracking icebergs and many other things.

I have dwelt briefly on these topics only because I want to refer in more detail to the development of the first one, communications satellites and to our old friend, the Space Shuttle.

The Space Shuttle is intended to put 65,000 lbs into orbit, from Cape Kennedy or 30,000 lbs into a polar orbit from the missile range at Vandenberg, the launching pad for the polar flights and for reconnaissance satellites. This pad is also used for the Lockheed Big Bird reconnaissance satellite. Among other things, it can return photographic capsules to earth from the Big Bird. So, although the intention is now to have a re-usable shuttle, the idea of actually returning something from space is not totally new. As most people know, the plan for the shuttle has recently been changed. It is now expected to reach forty launches a year from the Cape in the mid-eighties, and twenty launches a year from Vandenberg. That will require a fleet of five orbiters going backwards and forwards. Three will be based by NASA at the Cape and the other two with the US Air Force at Vandenberg.

The economic impact of this re-use of craft techniques is fascinating. The shuttle cuts the cost (or *should do* even though it has now been delayed) of each pound weight put into orbit. The original idea was to cut that cost from $1,000 a pound to about $100 a pound: that is an order of magnitude which really does open the application of regular space travel by a great factor.

Incidentally this month (July 1979) is also the tenth anniversary of a less glamorous and less exotic affair than the moon landing: it is the anniversary of the opening of the first public service earth station in the Middle East, at Bahrain. Earth stations are the unglamorous end of the business, that is unless they are attached to a network like Stanford University's. They are for interplanetary probes and for picking up signals down in the millionth of a watt area, signals that you can use for making those beautiful pictures of Mars and of Venus.

Then there is the Manpac portable variety, which is being used in an experiment with NATO and the American forces, using the navigation satellite for a platoon to be able to fix its position. They are enormously expensive, they are not the bread-and-butter game, but what I call a slightly more exotic and more interesting toy.

Most people are more familiar with the commercial variety, such as the standard 90-foot dish that we all know about down in places like Goonhilly and Bahrain.

Fifteen years ago the number of overseas telephone calls made from the Middle East was measured in three or four hundred a day. The current figure is about 250,000 a day, underlining the staggering impact of satellite communications. Similar expansion has been occurring in Africa, the Caribbean and other countries in the Pacific and Indian oceans.

The pace of development is even more remarkable considering that as late as 1965 there were only five satellite terminals in the United States and Europe for commercial communications. They were handling fewer than 100 telephone circuits between them. In 1980 there will be more than 5,000 circuits each capable of handling 240 two-way telephone channels to cope with the public service, and I stress the public service and not the private service, through eight satellites over the Atlantic, Indian and Pacific oceans.

Thus, five generations of communications satellites have evolved over that period plus a major modification of one of them. Table A is a breakdown of those five generations of satellites (or rather five plus the modification in the middle). The important point is the increase in power as they go up. However it is the bottom line that interests me. We have an enormous *decrease* in costs per circuit year that goes with the *increase* in the capacity of the satellite. Of course, the factors that combine to produce that particular ratio are many.

Table A. Four generations of satellites

Intelsat I	II	III	IV	IVA	V
1965	1967	1968	1971	1975	1979
59.6 cms	67.3	104	528	590	1,570
38 kgs	86	152	700	790	967
Thor-Delta	T–D	T–D	Atlas-Centaur	A–C	A–C
40 watts	75	120	400	500	1,200
50 MHz	130	500	500	800	2,300
240 telephone or 1 tv	240	1,200	4,000	6,000	12,000
1.5 design life years	3	5	7	7	7
Cost per circuit year $32,500	$11,400	$2,000	$1,200	$1,100	$800

We have come some way since Early Bird (or Intelsat I, to be more formal). That had one 240-telephone channel or one television channel (you could not have both). Now we have 12,000 circuits in the operational Intelsat Vs.

The critics in the early days who believed the idea of satellite communications was a technical luxury have been confounded by the way demand continues to push the technology. The Intelsat Annual Report in June 1979 states, 'Capacity rose by 25 per cent last year'. And an Intelsat Conference on Global Traffic Planning that took place recently projects that the rise will be another 100 per cent by 1983.

Last year (1978) the occasional television services (which is what the television services are) increased by 50 per cent. In practical terms that meant more than 11,600 channel hours. That demand was boosted by World Cup football transmissions. The estimate was that over 3,200 hours of transmission to more than one billion viewers took place at that time. That also I think might say something about the state of education in the world. Be that as it may, it is all good business, and that business is reflected in Table B.

Again I think the forecast is fairly self-explanatory. The reason why I have separated out the public service from the private line is perhaps a little more obvious now because you can see the private line requirement is at the top of the table. But what is extraordinary is the increase in the demand for earth stations. Categories One and Two are in fact the International Satellite Organisations Standard A and Standard B. Category One are fairly large public service stations that are going to be run by the PTTs, Post Office, Cable and Wireless, AT&T and organisations like that. The smaller earth stations —Category Two — run into these very large numbers. These include the direct broadcasting ones; the receive-only stations that are going to be built in the Indian sub-continent, throughout the Arab world, Africa, Latin America, countries

Table B

Type of market	1978	1980	1983	1985
Private line	$30 m.	$60	$200	$1,100
Broadcasting services	$40	$65	$90	$200
Satellites for com. delivered	2	5	8	5
Earth stations				
Category 1	2,000	3,600	7,700	12,000
Category 2	50	350	525	1,400
Total business	$168 million	$278 million	$498 million	$1.5 billion

Category 1 receive only at $3,000 to $10,000
Category 2 receive–transmit stations, $3 million to $8 million.

where there will be organisations that want to do direct broadcasting. The whole issue of direct broadcasting, and the politics of direct broadcasting and the issue of what happens when people start to broadcast over territorial boundaries without agreement, is obviously a very explosive and emotional issue.

This equipment can in fact be broken down into a number of applications. Some of them would be regional satellites like the Arab states, the Latin American world, the African world. There will be developments like video-conferencing, the SBS (Satellite Business System) service for high-speed data, facsimile transmission, the bulk of which is taken up by the private line figure at the top. What interests me on the technical side is how the powers that be are going to resolve the problem of flinging many more satellites into space. Because it actually is already creating congestion: the notion of how internationally we treat the geo-synchronous orbit as an international resource is one that is far, far from being resolved.

It has been an immense jump since the launch of the first passive reflector balloons such as ECHO, and it is an even bigger jump to the idea of launching by Shuttle instead of by expandable launchers.

Later we shall have Phase Two or Phase Three, of the Shuttle. Once they get it off the ground, they will be carrying a pay-load that actually has a small rocket unit attached to it that will take a satellite into another orbit. As one American I talked to recently, working in the satellite field, said, 'Those orbiting birds in the sky are becoming the golden geese'.

PART FIVE
Introduction

We come at last, without any disrespect to those who have written in previous pages, to the section which the editor considers to be the heart of this book.

I commented earlier that computing related interests dominated the proceedings: they have echoed throughout the preceding pages. Computing in turn leads to machine intelligence, and that I wrote is an area where science fact and science fiction meet. Machine intelligence however one has to remember is, in more than embryonic form, still in the future.

How such intelligence might behave was quickly touched on by Frank George. But will it, can it, exist? If so, in what form? And what might we do with intelligent machines? Such questions are central to what follows.

We begin this final section with a contribution by Tony Buzan which in some ways can be said to negate these issues almost in their entirety. The Buzan thesis is that we are provided by nature with very powerful computing engines, engines called brains which are hardly ever fully utilised.

They are as he shows remarkable engines. Only after the conference was over did it become apparent that one paper we needed was one which speculated on man machine symbiosis, one which took the forecast technology and asked what might happen were we to utilise our brains in the way that Tony Buzan describes in conjunction with ultra intelligent machines. It may well be, indeed probably is, that the fully stretched brain acting jointly with an ultra intelligent machine has a promise which we can only dimly foresee.

But do we have to wait for either? Heinz Wolff in his second contribution shows how inventive the human mind at its best can be and how much we could do without waiting for any massive changes to be brought about by the application of technology, smart machines or no.

Now take a world in which there is a better use of human wit and existing resources and add to it the technology foreseen by Earl Joseph. It is a very different view to that usually portrayed, in that as Joseph points out economics dictate not simply intelligent devices in one or hundreds, but in millions. It is an anti-centralist world, one in which the tools for survival, change and progress are not concentrated on and with the powers that be, but are available, indeed have to be available to the rest of us. It is a heartening vision, yet one rooted in economic reality.

Its time scale is the near future: the next fifty years. By contrast the editor's own paper looks at the situation a thousand years on, using the device of a lecturer looking back at our own world and commenting on the differences between the two.

There was no prior collaboration between the two authors on these papers. Yet they both share something in common: computing or whatever it will be called in the future will be accessible to all. And the consequences of that are radical in the best sense of that overworked word.

11 THE BRAIN

Tony Buzan

Tony Buzan is Director of the Learning Methods Group. He is the author of five books on the brain and brain application techniques and of a number of television programmes, including the 10 part BBC educational series, 'Use Your Head'.

There are brains in the universe that can detect the minutest changes in light, the minutest changes in sound, smell and touch. That can delicately and accurately integrate the actions of many muscles. That can regulate the functions of their bodies' many organs so as to preserve the optimum conditions for their own particular life. These brains also learn from experience. They have found ways to communicate with each other and they use languages to do that. They also share knowledge. They are sensitive to magnetic and electrical fields and also to ultra-violet light. They can analyse the polarisation of sunlight and can use it to tell directions. They keep a constant track of time throughout the cycles of their day and night and function as accurate guidance systems. They can land instantaneously on moving objects with superb accuracy. These brains are the brains of bees. They are less than the size of a grain of salt and contain 900 neurons; 900 brain cells.

The human brain is millions of times larger than those systems and billions of times more complex. What I want to do is to discuss our present knowledge of the human brain, and the futures that are possible for our brains.

I will explain why a system which seems to be so complex and amazingly beautiful can perform inadequately on so many fronts. I shall start with the history of our knowledge of the brain and then give you some indications of where the new research is going, what the findings are, and what this suggests for the future.

We can begin by placing our knowledge into a useful time context by considering a number of dates in the history of the universe. The first one, of course, is when was the universe created? There are two major schools of thought on that; either it has been there for ever (the timescale being infinity) or approximately twenty thousand million years.

The next date I would like to consider is the generally assumed date of the creation of the planet Earth and the solar system, which is around five thousand million years ago.

Next, the creation of life. This occurred four to four and a half thousand million years ago, very very close to the time when the planet was formed.

I then want to make another large jump to the arrival on the planet of *Homo sapiens*, which was between two and five million years ago, the current best estimate. We have dropped down from four thousand million to perhaps two to five million since we as a species have been on the planet. Now, the next leap I want to make is a debatable one: when did civilisation arrive? Many people would say that as yet it has not. But one of the standard estimates is ten thousand years.

I next want to jump to our knowledge of where the brain is located. This is a serious question. Is it in the head? Some people will say it is in another part of the anatomy, but it is basically in the head. Now, you know that because that is what you have been told. Supposing, just for a moment, you tried to imagine that you did not know where your brain was, and you had to decide where the seat of your emotions, your sexual drives, your mentation, your memory, your imagination, was; how would you work it out and what probable conclusion would you come up with? All over? Top half? Subjectively there? Outside the body? Heart? The whole lot. That actually was a brief summary of what scientists, and philosophers and 'psychologists', in early civilisations thought. Most of them, since the time of Aristotle, assumed that most of the functions we now know to be in the brain were in the heart. That is a very rational decision, because when you get emotional the heart reacts by beating faster. You stick something through the heart and there is no life. You stick something through somewhere else and you can survive. So it was assumed that what we call brain functions took place in the heart. And it is in fact only in the last (here is another debatable range) five hundred to one thousand years that we as a race have even known where what we are, in a sense, was centered.

The next jump is to talk about when most of the information that we have about that centre was found. The answer, of course, is in the last ten years. It is conservatively estimated that 95 per cent of all the information that we as a race have ever had about our brains has been found in the last ten years. It is further estimated that what we know at the moment is far less than one per cent of what there is to know. What we actually use is probably less than one per cent of its real capability. We are really still almost totally ignorant about what we are and in fact we hardly use the brain at all.

I would like now to introduce you to a few of the new bits of information — and I use 'bit' in the large sense here — that have been found in some of the laboratories around the world about the brain and what implications there seem to be for the future.

The first piece of research I want to discuss was carried out by Robert Ornstein at the University of California. Now one of the science fiction ideas of the past was the fact that we had brainwaves. That has now been proven: we do have brain waves and they are measurable. Ornstein was simply playing with brainwave machinery in California, trying to establish what kind of brainwaves were coming off for what kind of mental activity. To do this you give people a plastic cap with electrodes which measures the different kind of brainwaves which the brain gives off. There are some waves if you are doing mathematical tasks, others if you are listening to music, etc. Ornstein was asking people to do various exercises and monitoring the brain waves that were coming off. He found a result for which he was completely unprepared, and was till then unthought of. This concerned the two sides of the brain. If you are looking at the brain from above it is divided into two halves joined by a phenomenally complex network of nerves called the *corpus callosum*. There is a left and a right side to the brain.

What Ornstein found, and I emphasise that this was a surprise, was that the brainwaves that were coming off when people were doing these different activities were different; different from either side. So that when a person was doing mathematics a whole group of waves that indicate mathematics were coming off, but only from one side of the brain. Similarly when they were listening to music, again brainwaves were coming off but only from one side, and the other side seemed to go into a meditative 'hum' state. He researched and researched and found a general division of activities which could be roughly summarised as follows. The left side of the human brain, on average, is concerned with the following major mental areas: logic, language, number, linearity, sequence, etc.: the activities we call academic or scientific. While those activities were going on, the right side of the brain seemed to be asleep. The right side became very active and the left side went into a 'hum' during the following activities: rhythm, music, colour — any appreciation of colour, what I will call dimension — seeing things spatially rather than in two dimensions, day-dreaming, etc.: the so-called artistic activities.

He found this to be true of a person, regardless of how they described themselves. So the person said, I am marvellous at rhythm, music, and artistic things, but I am useless over there. As long as they were given these kinds of things to do that side of the brain seemed to take over and do it. This meant that the self-description did not seem to coincide with the physiological fact of the matter. There also did not seem to be much difference between the two sides of the brain. It is a mirror for all intentional purposes, so there was equal physical division of the organ.

What Ornstein and others with him decided to do was to train people on their weak sides. In other words, encourage them in that which was least strong. What he expected was a one-plus-one relationship. He thought that if he trained the weak side of the brain and then gave people general tests, they would double their overall ability. But that was not the result at all! He very often obtained results of 5+ times better, the creativity score, productivity, and so forth zooming up. The question is why should that have happened? Information is sent across the central nerve path zone (this is simplifying it obviously), considered and sent back. And so it is bigger. This is then sent back again, and becomes larger and so on. It develops if you like, almost a conversation within itself; a growing up and exchange of information. It builds as it goes along.

There were two very strong chunks of evidence for this theory. First the pure brainwave evidence, second the fact that when people were trained in an area in which they thought they were weak they improved enormously overall. There seemed to be contrary evidence, however, and that came from history. Looking at the great brains of history, one could fairly well divide them into these divisions, which seemed to indicate that they were not, if you like, balanced minds.

So they looked again at the great minds. Einstein obviously would be on what side? Left. Picasso, Paul Klee and so on on the Right. They investigated the lives of the great scientists and great artists. You find that Albert Einstein failed mathematics when he was in school. Imagine the report card: 'Little Albert is no good at sums, do not recommend a career in the sciences'. Brain stamped out. His hobby was the violin and sailing. Right side of the brain. He was also partially involved in art.

If you take, say, the drawings of Paul Klee and you look at the notebooks, you find that the artist will be saying things like: 'I was measuring 4.3 parts of this colour to 7.2 parts of this, in order to give this colour combination, which I place at this junction on the canvas to act in opposition to this colour combination down here, placed there.' Pure physics. And the more the great brains have been investigated, the more we find that they have been misdescribed. The pictures that you get in your science books and your history books are all one-sided. They were not like that. If you read Newton's discovery of the rainbow, it's like a child in a toyroom, just phenomenal imagination. He was out there in the country playing around with bits of broken glass. And then he put his linearity, his order into his imaginative discovery.

Einstein, particularly, when he was discovering his theory of relativity, said that one of the major break-throughs that he had mentally was not sitting in his laboratory doing his 'academic work', but lying on a hill on a summer's day, flat on his back, looking up at the sky and he suddenly wondered what it would be like to be on the surface of the sun — assuming that you were temperature proof — and to go for a ride on a sunbeam. So off he went, on a little ride, and he ended up where he started, which was illogical. His science had taught him that that was impossible. So he got on another sunbeam, off he went in his imagination. And again he came back. He describes that part of his thought process in the sense of having had the image and the imagination. He then wrapped around it the language, the symbol, the number, the code, the formula to describe the image, the conception that he actually had. So again, it was a balancing process.

Most of the information that is coming out of the laboratories at the moment, and out of schools and universities is finding when the activities of the brain are balanced, the whole thing improves. Phenomenally. If a person is good at number and then starts to practice music, for example, the numerical ability improves as well as, of course, the musical ability. So you have this synergy, producing these kinds of results immediately. This of course has a large number of implications for behaviour, education, personal function and so on.

In terms of education, if you were in your first week of school, say at the age of five, and you exhibited great talents for day-dreaming, for tapping out rhythms on the desk, for making imaginative comments in the class, and you could build things with your hands, how were you described? Thick, unintelligent, wrong, disruptive, and so on and so forth. That side of the brain literally would be destroyed.

Now, how many people would have normally described themselves as not particularly good at art, i.e. drawing, colour, dimensions, and reproducing images on paper? How many people would have similarly described themselves as not particularly good at mathematics, number? Those are the two main 'I cannot do it' syndromes. How do you know you cannot do it? Because you have done badly. It is proven, isn't it? If you sit there and you are doing your mathematics to begin with, and somebody else does better than you do, then it is up front that they have done better and you have done worse. This is your first time. What is your likely reaction going to be, the next time you go to the mathematics class? I am going to fail, I do not like it, I am not interested; and so one negative which is placed onto a system which is as sensitive as the brain can destroy it in that area for the rest of its existence. One well-placed negative can wipe it out in that particular area. Now this piece of information relates enormously to the whole idea of writing science fact/fiction. Because in these terms, scientific and artistic are not opposites, they are in fact the same. The great artist is by definition a scientist. The great scientist is by definition an artist. Now, with this information, it is possible that we can improve creativity enormously.

When, then, is creative activity most likely to happen? What physical position do you find yourself in when you are having the birth of generally creative, imaginative ideas and thoughts? Driving, sitting in a moving vehicle, on the toilet, walking, in the bath, dozing behind the desk with your eyes closed. What kind of situations is one physically in when, if you like, right-side of the brain functions are taking place? Relaxed and very often alone, which suggests that if you want the whole brain to function and to be in synchrony with itself (almost a breathing function if you like) it is necessary to organise time so that it is different; that your activities are not always left-logical but are often right — rest-relaxed. Therefore, in terms of any generally working or personal function, it is essential to have regular rest, regular breaks; because when you do that you are actually getting the full brain working. If you do not do it you are actually almost, in the real sense of the term, a half-wit because there is only one side of the brain which is being used. So, let that right one go . . .

Another popular assumption currently under challenge is that we think in linguistic grammatical, sentential ways. Thinking is far more associative. Associations are made between bits of information in the brain which include words, numbers, images, and your senses. One can think of each unit of information, like a word, like a thought, like a number, as a spherical centre from which extend thousands of connective possibilities. Associations, if you will. This is the substance of 'information in your brain', and it includes words, numbers, it includes images, and all of your senses. Each item has that spray of associations, and this is in your brain as it operates at the moment. So we can say that each and every unit is individual, in other words it is personally yours. But not only is it individual, it is *extremely* individual, and extremely is perhaps the key word. Every word, every number, every image, every sense, every idea is extremely individual and while it has some connections with ideas of other people, basically it is *different*.

What does this mean in terms of the way the brain functions, language, thought and so on. A number of things. First of all it challenges what I would call the popular assumption of the way in which we think, and that being linguistic, grammatical, and in sentences. It suggests that thought is far more associative, that associative is a key word. You can check the degree to which the brain depends on sentence and grammar for memory, by trying a little exercise. It is not a test but an exercise in introspection. Consider all the sentences that you have ever been in contact with, for your entire life. Now, by contact I mean every sentence you have spoken, listened to, read or thought; all of them. Subtract from those, any sentence of ten words or less. This will probably leave you with about half of them, which will be those sentences of eleven words or more. There will be tens of millions of them. Subtract from those tens of millions only the few hundred which you have memorised, in things like prayers or songs, special bits of poetry or your favourite bits of writing. You are now left with all the sentences you have ever spoken, read, written or absorbed in any other way (with the exception of things which you have specifically memorised). Now write down ten of them, just ten, word perfectly. Ten sentences from your entire life-time that you have read, spoken, listened to or written, that are eleven words or more in length, and there are tens of millions for you to choose from.

As you try it, think about how your brain works. Think about what is actually being remembered while you try, don't try to think of reasons why you are not remembering them, think of what happens when you try to.

Not an easy task. Let's look at the kind of process going on while you were trying to remember the sentences. What did you remember if it was, say, to begin with, not a sentence? Visual scenes, ideas, going back into a role. In the last few years it has been shown that basically the brain does not use sentences for memory purposes. It can remember them, but it is much more stressful than to remember by a central node whether that be a word, an image, an idea or whatever, which is then connected to something else. Each individual does it differently, but using the same process.

Does this piece of information have any implications in terms of changing behaviour, raising levels of consciousness — if you like — adapting education, changing the way in which communication normally works, adapting it to business situations, etc. Knowing that each bit of information is a unit which is uniquely individual, and has a number of associative possibilities; it becomes the key to memorisation. If you want to remember, start to make associations.

How, and what kinds of associations should one try to make? We are talking here specifically about memory. Make right-brained associations, get in as much image sense, emotional feeling as you can, and your memory rockets. It will improve on simple tests by very large factors.

The experiments that have been done on this have shown that if you know how to do it properly, and if you give yourself a bit of training in imaging, you can memorise a list of a thousand items perfectly. And somebody can ask, what was number 725, and you say what it is. No problem with it at all, if one uses the brain as I suggest it was designed to be used.

It seems that the potential of your brain in a certain number of areas may well be infinite, in terms of its own particular life span. Retention, which is the act of storage; and recall, the getting back of it. We know that the brain can do that perfectly for a life-time. There is now no doubt about that. There are, and have been throughout history, a series a individuals who did not seem to be any different from others in most ways — with the exception of the fact that they could remember everything. The most well documented case is that of a man called 'S', in Russia, who was found in Moscow one day in an editorial meeting, not taking notes from the editor. They asked him why he did not take notes, because it was a crucially important meeting; he became embarrassed because he did not understand what notes were for.

He had always felt that there was something wrong with him, that other people had this skill and they were all doing these things that he did not really understand. He finally explained that he could remember it anyway, so they challenged him and he just stood up and gave it. Word for word. He was then rushed off to Moscow University, and given to Professor Luria to study. Luria spent 15 years studying this man. The first test that he did with him was saying something like this, 'I want you to listen to what I am going to say and repeat it.' And he went on for about 15 minutes, reading out, and then said, 'what did I say'. 'S' said, 'well quite obviously . . .' and repeated the whole lot. If you asked this man questions like what were you doing 15 years ago, on January 2nd, he could scratch his head and say, what time? His brain had literally documented every event.

Work by people like Penfield, who has also suggested that by the correct stimulation of electrodes memories from the entire lifetime come back, and not only come back as a memory but if they are stimulated direct, they come back as new existence. In other words, if we did it with each one of us, ten years from now, and we hit the right section of your brain, you would feel you were back here. If somebody asked you where you were, you would say, back here. If they asked you to look around, you would look around and you would see whatever is around you right now. Total memory. And the suggestion coming out of the labs at the moment is that memory seems to be potentially perfect; it is just a matter of training it.

Hypnotism can do the same kind of thing, and so can the pre-death experience. If a man is falling off a 10,000 foot cliff, and he assumes that he is going to die, what happens? His whole life goes in front of him. This is the standard response. And if you ask him, was it not just the afternoon with Cecilia by the sea, or something, he says no, and insists that it was the entire thing, that time stood still and he saw everything at the one instantaneous moment. Why that happens may be that under that shock the energy of the entire system is total. It is the last, final, complete if you like, shocking review. In terms of memory and creativity, it is now being suggested that learning can go on and on and on. Any child, as long as it understands the way it associates and memorises, can get 100 per cent in most standard exams. There is no difficulty in absorbing the information, it is simply absorbing it in a way in which the brain is designed to do it.

There is a man called Suzuki, in Tokyo, who was a violinist and he had a friend who was a violin maker. He noticed that the Japanese were able to train songbirds by hatching new birds in the presence of a master singer. Every new bird learned to sing the master's song, regardless of its parentage. They thought, well if a bird-brain can mimic the best, and then go off on its own particular creative processes, what could a human brain do? So he got his friend to make violins for children's arms, so they were not playing double basses, and he just sat down in the middle of the floor and played his own violin with two, three, four year old children. There are now tens of thousands of children around the world who learn music in the way that we learn language. Music is simply another language. Any child learns to speak the languages that are around it. If there are three languages around it, it speaks three. And if there is violin playing around it, it plays the violin, as long as it is allowed to mimic, to pace itself, to learn and, especially, to be loved and cared for during the time that it is doing that learning. All these suggestions indicate that the potential of the brain is hundreds and hundreds of times better than we thought.

At the moment we are operating on a series of evolutionarily defined ignorances, we take notes in the way we have been trained to take notes, we do not use colour, we do not think we can do things and so on and so forth. But if we were properly taught, then the utopias in which people could really use this wonderful thing, the brain, and understand each other more adequately and create, and learn, could be realised.

12   MAN MACHINE SYMBIOSIS

Heinz Wolff

Let me begin by issuing an intellectual challenge to Earl
Joseph and Tony Buzan: I wish to point out an apparent
paradox. They both make statements to the effect that a
human brain contains some very large number of elements,
each of which may be equivalent to any number of gates,
and that in practice at present we appear to use only a very
small proportion of these. The question that I would like to
pose is this: why has evolution, usually so economical,
equipped us with so vast an over-capacity, most of which
does not appear to have any survival value? Indeed, it
presents a puzzle which I would like explained.

I would like to throw out one possible explanation, this
is that it is at least possible that both of them overestimate
the steepness of the relationship between the number of
elements and the increase in computing power. The hundred
billion elements may not in any sense represent the gain in
computing power which linear extrapolation would tend to
suggest. The reasons for this may for instance be that a lot
of redundancy is needed to insure oneself against failure; or
that it may be useful to store information in lots of different
forms so that it can be accessed from different directions, its
unique storage in one place should necessitate rather complex
access methods. We know that information is stored to some

extent in a disseminated way in the brain, it is not in single cells. So I would like to ask Tony Buzan, whether he is really sure that we do only utilise such a small proportion of our brains or whether, in fact, it is not back-up; necessary to us as a species, if not as individuals. And I would like just to question, therefore, whether the technology improvements are likely to produce anything resembling the sort of gain in computing performance that was suggested.

Secondly, I would like to comment on Dr. Joseph's hopeful and immensely heartening ideas. He has put to us the picture of distributed essential facilities. I think he might have gone a little far by suggesting a machine which actually made cornflakes in the fields. Nevertheless, the concept that it may be desirable and possible to have distributed facilities of all kinds, from those which manufacture things to those which generate power, takes care very nicely of the danger I feared, the danger to the stability of society presented by a high degree of concentration of facilities and therefore a high possibility of disruption by malcontents. Whatever their motives, the ability of a small number of people to disturb the system to the detriment of society as a whole seems to me to be an entirely undesirable effect of high technology. If Earl Joseph assures me that we may well have the possibility to move in the direction of distributed capability then I find this very heartening.

I would like now to list the overt demands of society, what facilities it actually feels the need for, and then to deal with some of them in greater detail. I have put these very roughly in what I regard as a priority order, though you may disagree with the ordering.

We obviously want food, and some form of shelter. We want life-long health and security; the security of being looked after when we are ill. I maintain that we want work, or an occupation of some kind, and this work or occupation may well contain an element of competition and provide an avenue to individual success. Perhaps more controversially, I think that we put a very high value on the availability of personal or near-personal transport. Connecting people by cables so that they do things in their homes and do not have the social benefits of moving around and going to the shops or the office, where they meet other people and feel and touch and smell other people, seems to me to be entirely cloud-cuckoo land. Therefore, whatever the fuel may be, I think there will always be an industry which moves people about and this will be a high priority.

It is known from studies of the deprived in the United States that families well below the poverty line will still maintain a motor car, even if it means that all sorts of other things go by the board, including the nutrition of the family. So I would maintain that the attainment of mobility over one's medium range environment, at the time when one wants it, is something we regard as important. It may be tendentious to say this, but in those countries which we regard as relatively unfree there is in fact little availability of personal transport under one's own control; the two things appear to go together.

The next requirement on my list is things to do in your leisure. I think we may well find that in the future there is a trade-off between competitiveness at work and the competitiveness of excelling at something in your leisure. Instead of becoming powerful at work it may be just as satisfying to have a certificate hanging in one's office, as I do, 'Wolf Cub's Fathers' Sack Race — first prize — 1963.'

Lastly, and I quite deliberately put it last, is the requirement for education. To prevent misunderstanding, I repeat that these are *overt* requirements, these are what the customer thinks he wants, in the order in which I think he wants them. I would guess (and this is the only pessimistic note which I am going to voice) that as work becomes less essential, so the demand for education will drop. There is at the moment a fair correlation in many people's minds beween a good job and being educated. If the necessity for work decreases we may also find that the demand for education decreases. Idyllic desert islands where the coconuts fall off the trees, and bananas are to be had for picking are not notable for running high-powered schools or investing a great deal of effort in education. We may be different about this, but it may well require a form of religious conversion, a missionary zeal, to get people to continue to put a high priority on education when the vocational aspects become less important.

Now I am going to analyse four or five of the requirements I have listed, with considerable emphasis on how technology might affect them in the short-term, i.e. within the next twenty, thirty or fifty years.

I am afraid that after all I have to sound a second pessimistic note. When I talk about us, in the plural, I talk about Europe and the developed world. I do not believe that in this short-term future we will make a very large impression, however hard we try, and however hard we ought to try, on the problems of the Third World. Their problems are too large, and whilst we might help in a number of ways, I do not believe that the Third World within this thirty year time scale is going to be very much better off than it is at present.

Let us take this first requirement, food. Food availability depends on two factors, how much you grow (there is obviously room for improvement in this, which is not, strictly speaking, the subject of this conference) and how many people there are to eat it. It is a truism to say that in the Third World they cannot catch up on themselves, that populations are expanding at a rate that keeps pace with, or is even faster than, their increasing ability to grow food. So population control is very important. And this, unfortunately, is not a question of contraception; so much is known about contraception that there is not really any need for anybody in the world not to know how not to have a baby. But unfortunately in a country like India, where there is no social insurance, the only way of not starving when you are old is to make sure you have enough sons to look after you. This is a very uneconomic way of taking out social security. And unless this vicious circle can be broken, where people can only insure themselves for the future by having a large number of children, and the large number of children in effect eat up the future, there is no real way of helping them. It would take a generation of changing attitudes before the attitude that it is a good thing to have lots of sons was modified. It is for this reason that I cannot see a short-term solution to the problems of population, as far as the Third World is concerned.

In my own laboratories we are actually doing something about contraception. As this is being done under a World Health Organisation contract and as we have been asked to get Patent Protection I cannot go into it in very great detail. But physiologically the female body produces a number of signals which can be picked up from the outside comparatively easily, whose rhythms coincide with the menstrual rhythm. To plot graphs of these rhythms is not the kind of thing you can easily do in a mud hut. However, it is possible to produce a cheap device which can pick up one or more of these signals and do the plotting for you. It can include an algorithm to identify the changes coincident with ovulation, so that the woman can identify that time of the menstrual cycle when intercourse would not be followed by conception. It should identify a good deal more accurately than the common method the so-called 'safe' period. It does not involve hormones, nor the introduction of any device into the body. It is voluntary. It allows people to control the spacing of their own pregnancies and, used on a village or a town scale, it will affect the overall birth rate. Even if it were wrong on one occasion in twenty, it would still make a very significant impact on the population of a society.

This device involves electronics, a mixture of micro-processor and a bit of memory, because it has to store some program for the algorithm: it stores information which it picks up throughout the cycle and it communicates either its decision, or the evidence on which the individuals themselves can take the decision. How the presentation of the results of such a device should actually occur is still a moot point.

The requirement of personal transport I am not going to say much about. Whether it is mopeds or cars or some form of public transport passing your house every two minutes, in principle does not matter. The only important fact is that this is going to be an enduring industry and we shall want to use an appreciable part of our resources to satisfy this parti-cular human whim.

Entertainment and leisure also I am going to pass over very quickly, so as to concentrate my particular concerns on health and security. Entertainment and leisure are im-portant. Most of us agree that there will be less productive work to be done and that people will spend more time 'doing their own thing'. As I have already said, I think it is a very important part of ensuring a happy society to provide as many ways as possible in which people can excel as indi-viduals. This can just as easily be in the leisure field as it can be in the work field. It could well be that the devising of games and sports of all kinds (which can have hidden inside them a technological content) may turn out to be not just good business, but also a factor which stabilises society. If they open up avenues to things which people can be good at, they can be important for people's self-respect.

I put education down low on the list of what the consumer wants. This does not mean I put it low on the list of what I think society may want to provide. I said previously that I thought there was a danger that unless we pumped in education we might, in a sense, disenfranchise people, because they would not be able to understand what contemporary problems were about and therefore could not have an opinion: they would be in the hands of whoever wanted to manipulate them. The only way we can counteract this is by education. I was not very happy about the idea of the school on a wafer, because to me education, at least at the seminal stage when people are being taught how to learn, is not like this. You do not actually learn anything very much at school: what you learn is how to become a social animal, and how to acquire information. I maintain that this can only be done by people. Learning how to become a social animal requires contact between the little animals, in a classroom, in the care of one or more other people. Moreover it requires the devising of as many ways of putting fundamentals into people as there are people!

I now come to health and security. I'm going to tell you about a new industry, the 'Tools for Living' Industry. It has become quite a hobby horse of mine and I have been given quite a lot of money to do something about it.

In all of the developed societies between fourteen and twenty per cent of the population are above retiring age, let us say above sixty-five. By and large jobs are no longer available for these people, and both their physical capabilities, and, as they get older, their mental capabilities, are decreasing. They are becoming increasingly disabled. This does not mean that three of you have not got grandmothers of 85 who are as nippy as birds and as bright as crystal, but on average there is a decrease in one's capabilities as one gets older. Now the necessity of coping with problems of ageing is relatively recent; animals on the whole do not live long enough to become senile, they get eaten by something or fall over a cliff. So my thesis is this: civilisation so far has done rather a good job at providing us with a tool kit for childhood, perambulators and toys and things of this kind, it has done well in providing us with a tool kit for our productive working life, machinery, computers and so on, but it has done almost nothing to provide us with a tool kit for our old age, for the third part of our life.

Last week I had a puncture in my car. I was standing there trying to lift the car up, and it was too heavy for me: I was disabled. Disability simply means inability to cope with some challenge which life issues to you. So, what do I do? Very fortunately, in the boot of my car I have a jack. I use a tool to help me, it makes me 'able' again. I lift my car, I change my wheel and I am off. So, because I am a tool-using animal I am able to extract myself from this particular situation. Now, I am trying to create a situation where the inabilities, or the decreasing abilities, of old age should be just as susceptible to being removed by the provision of suitable tools, as are the inabilities of childhood or the inabilities of adult life.

This should have nothing whatever to do with medicine. When you find that your finger is too blunt to drill a hole through a board, you do not go to your General Practitioner and get him to prescribe an electric drill for you. You go into the local do-it-yourself shop and you buy it. I would like to create a situation where this becomes possible over a fair range of non-medical disabilities. I do not mean that you should go to a supermarket and buy your pace-maker or your own artificial limb, but that there are an enormous host of devices where it is well within the ability of the individual, or the individual's relatives, to choose the appropriate tool which is required to *enable* the individual again.

How far is this possible at present? Quite a lot of people are one-handed not because of having a hand chopped off, but because of some condition like arthritis. They want to be able to feed themselves. Figure 1 shows a device which stops the plate from sliding about, and a clever knife which makes it possible to cut up meat with one hand; with these two a person can regain a bit of independence.

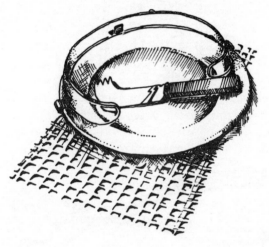

Figure 1

Figure 2 shows a raised lavatory seat for people who have difficulty getting up from a seated position. If you cannot go to the lavatory by yourself, you are totally dependent and somebody has to be there to look after you. Here is one thing that may make you independent for an extra year or two.

If you live in a wheelchair or are not very mobile, you need longer arms. Figure 3 is the best we can do at the moment, a set of tongs which give one an extra reach of

Figure 2

Figure 3

about 18 inches or so. It is not very clever because things slip out of it; but I can well imagine a version with a bit of 'sense' at its tips which will adjust the tightness of its grip according to the kind of surface it is gripping.

Shifting loads in the home can be a major problem. Mr. Jones, who weighs fifteen stone, has had a stroke which has left him with impaired mobility. His wife is bird-like, weighs eight stone, is as tough as old boots, but the one

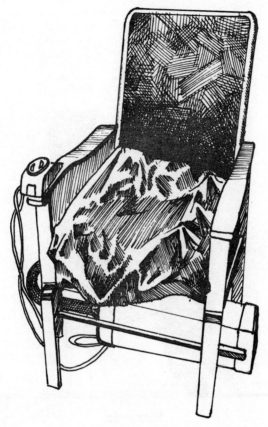

Figure 4

thing she cannot do is to lift him about. They require a
load-shifting piece of apparatus. Figure 4 shows a very
simple one, a plastic bag which goes underneath the cushion
of a chair and can be inflated with an abbreviated vacuum
cleaner. Without any gears or chains to snag his clothes,
Mr. Jones can be lifted in his chair. The whole technology

F.I.   M

Figure 4a

of using inflatables to get people in and out of baths, of chairs, of bed, is an almost unexploited industry.

If things get worse Mr. Jones may actually need a crane. Figure 5 shows one that has been installed in certain homes to make the transfer between bed and wheelchair possible without having to draft in outside help.

One of my favourite classes of aid is the psychotherapeutic aid, which enables somebody to continue some symbolic

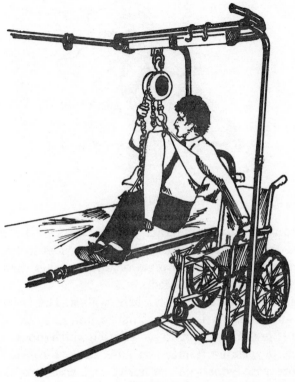

Figure 5

action which gives them some personality. Figure 6 shows a device which has been used ever since Victorian days for supporting the weight of a teapot leaving the operator only to provide the small forces required to pour a cup of tea.

In ergonomic terms this is not very important, but to grandma who is only visited every fortnight by her children, and wants to sit at the top of the table and perform the symbolic action of pouring the tea, rather than leaving it to her daughter-in-law (with whom she never got on) it may make the difference between being reasonably contented and

Figure 6

feeling unnecessary and rather less contented. The insight required to construct a wide variety of devices to keep the meaning in people's lives, badges of office, rather than tools for living, is almost unexplored.

Figure 7 shows a child with a baby walker. This is regarded as a lovely thing. It is a toy. You do not go to the doctor to have it prescribed. But to get a device which looks exactly the same, a walking frame, you have to go through a long procedure with your local authority and your hosptial and your occupational therapist.

These 'Tools for Living' should be treated as do-it-yourself tools, extensions of the tool kit you have acquired through life to help you through your old age.

So, what am I actually saying? I am saying that we are going to see a contraction of industry in certain sectors, like the motor car industry, upon which we depend quite heavily for employment and for the creation of wealth. We shall, however, have a new factor, that people above retiring age, because of occupational pension schemes, will have more money to spend than hitherto. And of course, these people will in fact be us. Also, we have higher cultural expectations

Figure 7

than those of the present older generation. So we shall expect
life to be better for us. We shall, therefore, be a new kind of
consumer, providing a market for whom nobody at present
caters in any organised manner, and for which the majority
of products have not been identified.

We will have to distribute these products in a rather more
ethical way than we market other things, because the 'hard-

sell' is inappropriate for this situation. We want something like a 'Grannycare' shop, where a lot of these things are available, but where advice is also available, the kind of attention one could get at an old-fashioned chemist's if one said one had a headache; and one was not simply sold the most expensive pills, but was also given a certain amount of advice. We have to create an industry, and to create people to work in this industry. A good deal of this work will be at the face-to-face level, identifying the most appropriate devices, teaching people how to use them, installing them and servicing them. Very few of these jobs at present exist.

This brings me to the question, is there a place for sophisticated technology in this enterprise? In my own laboratories we are working on a system where we give people a tiny radio-transmitter, about the size of a match-box, which they carry on their person or very close to them; they might for intance put it on their bedside table. If any trouble occurs (short of unconsciousness, which we cannot as yet detect), falling down the stairs, getting locked in the toilet, just feeling too cold in bed, the person can, by pressing the button, send out a coded radio signal which makes their own telephone dial a special telephone number and identify itself. The telephone number is the number of a computer, which stores three other telephone numbers for each of up to 1000 clients; say the married daughter in the next street, the son at the other end of town, and as a fall-back the matron of an old people's home in the same city. It will ring these people up and produce a plain language message: Mrs. So-and-So is in trouble, will you please go and have a look. The recipient can let the computer know that they have understood the message, and are going to take some action, and the computer then goes and attends to the next one. This system will soon be in operation for an initial 36 patients, but we hope it will go on to a larger number in the very near future.

I am incubating something even more ambitious, which I call an 'Interactive Environment'. This is really Big Brother stuff. One of the most tiresome ways in which old people become disabled is that they lose their short-term memory. They can remember with crystal clarity what happened when they were a little boy of seven, but they cannot remember that they have just put a kettle on the stove. It is technically possible to arrange their environment so that every time they open the front door it says, 'Have you taken your key with you?', and every time they turn the electric cooker on it reminds them ten minutes later that perhaps something ought to be happening. There is no limit to the complexity of possible algorithms, including things like, 'if the bed becomes heavier but does not become warmer after a certain time, dial the emergency 'phone number', or saying 'It's three o'clock, time to take your medicine, dear'. We have taken this sufficiently seriously to get to the point of discussing what sort of voice we should use: should the person apparently be talking to himself, quite respectably, should it be his favourite grandchild who says 'goodnight' last thing at night, or should it be the authoritarian tones of his health visitor that tells him to take his medicine? There is no reason why it should always say the same things; it could say one day, 'It's time to take your medicine', and the next day, 'Haven't we forgotten something?', or even wait to discover whether the action is performed without a reminder. And, if necessary, it could have a small portable out-station for the person to take out with him, giving his name and address and where he intended going.

All this is certainly possible, and I intend to create something like it in the not too distant future. What I have no idea about is whether it is psychologically acceptable to be programmed, as it were, through one's day.

If I had control over what people should be taught in

schools of what their job was likely to be, when they grow up and have to earn their living, I would say that the vast proportion of them will be concerned with performing services for each other. Only a minority will actually work in a productive industry because it seems likely that it may be more efficient for production to be carried out by machinery. The employment-providing industries will be those where people interact with people, whether they teach each other things, or cut each other's hair, or paint each other's houses, or take care of each other. Looking after people in the third third of life can, I think, become a major industry. So what we ought to be organising in our schools is giving children the idea that the good jobs, the satisfying jobs, the prestige jobs, are in fact the jobs concerned with performing mutual services for one another.

Some people may say that this is economically impossible, we cannot afford it. However what we can afford is determined in the final analysis by how much wealth we produce as a country, and not by how many people happen to be concerned in the creation of this wealth. We are committed to keeping everybody eating. It does not actually matter whether we pay them for doing nothing, or whether we pay them for taking care of each other. It is my contention that jobs where people are of use to other people are not only non-divisive, they actually bind society together. They are among the most satisfying things man can do. And I think this may be the salvation in the industrial situation we have produced by introducing high technology into the productive processes, thus ousting the production worker. With the help of a Latin dictionary, I have coined a name for a new type of man. The unfortunate combination of the serpent and the apple turned innocent man into *homo sapiens*. Now we have the opportunity to use another major perturbation, the introduction of high technology, to turn *homo sapiens* into *homo curatio*, not 'wise man', but 'caring man'. And it is interesting to remember that the conversion of the cold, aggressive, wise or knowing man into caring man is the aim of most religions.

13 SCIENCE FACT — LOOKING FORWARD TO THE 80s AND 90s

Earl C. Joseph

INTRODUCTION

This paper extrapolates science fact for the next 100 years, rather than dealing with science fiction. From these trends, it discusses some specific futures relative to computers and society for the 1980 and 1990 decades. Computer systems and technology developments for the 1980s are expected to split along a multiplicity of lines — some revolutionary new directions are expected to emerge as well as evolutionary advancements of past trends are forecastable. Further, there is increasing forecasting evidence that future computer systems will be far more revolutionary in nature for the late 1980 decade, and the 1990s, than for the evolutionary developments expected in the early 1980s.

Many factors, including rapid semiconductor technology advances, movements into VLSI (very large scale integrated circuits), VHSI (very high speed integrated circuits) and beyond, smart machine applications, office-of-the-future trends, further application diversity and widespread proliferation resulting from considerably lower cost hardware, and

The views expressed in this paper are those of the author and do not necessarily represent the position of Sperry Univac Division, Sperry Corporation.

many other technological advancements, suggest the forcing of a multiplicity of changing patterns. That is, the future of computers is largely technology driven. However, forecasts based solely on the technological superiority of new and/or rapidly advancing technology could be grossly misleading and miss the mark for the future. Many societal forces for further change or stability, such as energy crisis considerations, growing worldwide political pressures and competition, new government policies and regulations, management and public acceptance of change, and others, all point toward altering the patterns of rapid technological change — that is, many non-technological considerations share in influencing the course future computer developments will travel. In turn, such non-technological trends impact directly on which course technological innovation will be encouraged, or discouraged, toward developing. In the main, however, many non-technological considerations can often, in retrospect, be shown to be technology speed-up factors — as is the case for the opportunities spawned by the many new computer applications resulting from the energy crisis. Conversely, in the short term, non-technological problem considerations can considerably slow the introduction of new technology and new systems.

The new computer revolution developing, that is measurable in picoseconds, sub-microns, and component systems, variously called the 'silicon revolution', 'micro-revolution', 'information age', etc., can be forecasted to develop even faster in the 1980s. We are at the threshold of 'next generation' technological developments for ushering in a new 'knowledge processing' era which goes far beyond the information processing and data processing eras now underway.

OPPORTUNITIES AND PROBLEMS

Primarily, the technology influencing factors and opportunities emerging and forcing new computer developments in the 1980 decade and beyond are covered here. Since no discussion of future computer developments is possible without examining technology trends, much of what follows deals with expected hardware technology futures, and the alternatives. However, software and 'societalware' increasingly paces the development of future computers and their applications; therefore, some trends in these important areas are also covered.

But perhaps more importantly, as computers become smarter, and move toward 'people amplifier appliances', cultural considerations can be forecasted to become paramount — though this paper will only touch upon such cultural considerations.

Some new directions for computers were initiated in the 1970 decade — microprocessors, the silicon (Chip) revolution, and the office-of-the-future are but three from a longer list. Further advances in these key areas, and others, will be mapped for the future in this paper. Additionally, in the 1980 decade new ground will be broken as the computer field revolutionarily bifurcates along some new directions — some of these will also be outlined as 'future history' in what follows, together with a forecasted trend as they are expected to evolve.

However, rapid advances in the computer field are developing a great multiplicity of directions, and thus this paper dealing with the long-range outlook in computer developments can only touch upon a few of the important directions that the future will follow. Many others will be equally important.

There are today a number of negative social aspects of

computing that are currently impacting future computer design, some are:

Experts required

Errors and faults (hardware and software)

'Creating unemployment' myth of automation (the displacement of people problem)

High cost of hardware and software

Invasion of privacy.

Each of these and others are creating, once a computer system is designed and in use, certain problems, taboos, and forbidden zones of usage. If ignored, these no-no's cause certain publics to react adversely to computers — and in some cases cause lauws to be passed limiting or controlling what can be done (and how) with computers. In turn, as these no-no's become visible to computer designers and managers applying computers, systems tend to be designed to avoid or eliminate the future possibility of their occurrence.

For example:

Social Problem	Impact on Future Computer Design	Social Impact of Future System
Requires Experts	Convivial System	Friendlier and easier to use
Faults and Errors	Fault-Tolerant Self-Repairable Fail-Safe	Error-free operation
Unemployment Myth of Automation	Scenarios of Desirable Futures (from computer usage)	Opportunities to generate a higher QOL for society and more jobs
High Cost of Hardware and Software	Micro systems, VLSI/ VHSI, Software cost in Hardware and Software Engineering	Lower cost computing — Displacement of people — Smarter computers and smart machines

TRENDS IN TECHNOLOGY

Almost from the beginning of transistor usage in the modern computer era, an unbroken trend has been maintained for significant improvements in hardware technology and the cost/performance of each new computer system introduced. Advancements in the fundamental underlying semiconductor technology are expected to continue throughout the 1980s, along the trend trajectory started in the early 1960 time-frame, and which has become well established in the 1970s (see Figures 1 and 2). Therefore, measurements of the coming decade, using this technological advance pipeline as a yardstick, point to forecasts of tremendous change — and further proliferation of computers and their usage, resulting from continued technological driven price erosions together with computer system performance enhancements. The capabilities and application of semiconductor chips ten years from now will go far beyond what is currently being anticipated by most engineers. Extrapolated trends of some expected short-range future revolutions (Figure 1) and long-range future computer developments are shown (Figure 2) together with a look at forecasted computer/micro-component complexity trends.

The four short-range future computer revolutions, shown in Figure 1, now visible for the 1980s, are mapped as to their expected leading edge of occurrence, major character-istics, and the resulting impacts for society and computer systems, are:

1. The component processor revolution, forecast to begin now (1979/80), starts with providing a basic building block for computers and communication systems, next generation LSI and VLSI hardware, intelligent or 'smart' machine products, people amplifier appliances, and digital automation for embedding in other machines to make them smarter. Eventually this will result in such components also becoming end products.

2. The component computer revolution is forecastable to start in the 1981/83 period (with early trial versions in 1980), provides the basic component for systems, made from VLSI

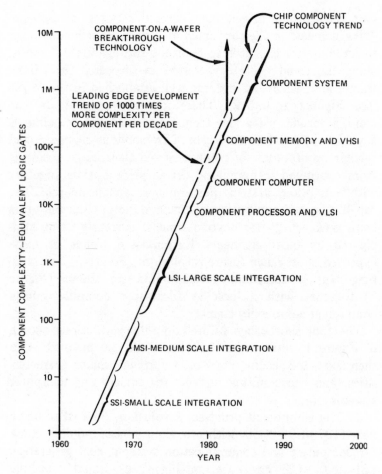

Figure 1 Computer/Micro Complexity Trend and Future
Revolutions — Component Computers

and VHSI hardware, and a progressively larger component
computer evolvable throughout the decade. It will be the era
of universal (rather than general purpose) computer products
and hard program products, leading to intelligent data

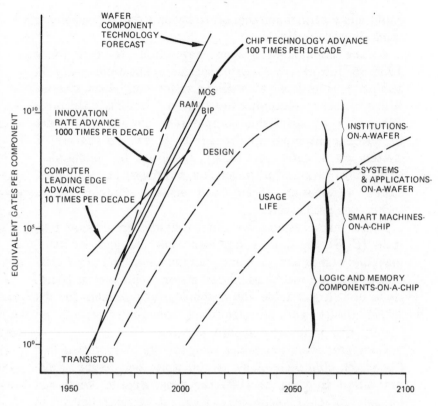

WAFER
COMPONENT
TECHNOLOGY
FORECAST

CHIP TECHNOLOGY ADVANCE
100 TIMES PER DECADE

MOS
RAM BIP

INNOVATION
RATE ADVANCE
1000 TIMES PER DECADE

DESIGN

COMPUTER
LEADING EDGE
ADVANCE
10 TIMES PER DECADE

USAGE
LIFE

INSTITUTIONS-
ON-A-WAFER

SYSTEMS
& APPLICATIONS-
ON-A-WAFER

SMART MACHINES-
ON-A-CHIP

LOGIC AND MEMORY
COMPONENTS-ON-A-CHIP

TRANSISTOR

EQUIVALENT GATES PER COMPONENT

10^{10}

10^5

10^0

1950   2000   2050   2100

Figure 2   Silicon Revolution: Future Forecast.

management systems and communications subsystem components. This development causes most computers to become components.

3. The component memory revolution forecast for a 1983/85 introduction kicks off with a basic memory building block for information systems, distributed memory, a system component for revolutionizing communications, information appliances, a smart database computer and knowledge based systems. This results in memory becoming components, and

could allow offices and schools to become portable machines some time in the 1990s.

4. The component systems revolution, forecast for a 1985/88 introduction (with special applications early in 1980/81), is initiated with silicon wafer component systems which further revolutionize institutions — leading to the possible demise of mainframe computers — and allows factories to become machines in the 1990s. It will be the era of 'system on a wafer' technology, there will be communications substitutions for travel and buildings, and the forecasted information society will emerge. Thus is future technology predictable.

From macrosystems to microsystems, an economy-of-scale (EOS) flip-flop: components become end products, machines/computers become components and factories/offices become machines. These major technological transitions now forecastable and technologically feasible for the 1980s future portend significant long-term impacts on society, and on future computer systems.

Computer evolution is increasing tenfold every decade (see Figure 2), chip technology at 100 times per decade, while innovation is going at 1000 times per decade. What will happen to chip technology when it 'crashes' into the computer curve? Will it bend toward the computer curve or will computers move onto the technology track? The answer is yes — to both questions!

New directions in microsystem technology will result in cybernetic machines: intelligent machines; people amplifier devices with para-expert adjuncts; information appliances; and microfactories or distributed factories.

This latter point needs elaboration. Imagine a future 'cookie farm'. The smart (computerized) planting machine loosens the land ultrasonically (or with short bursts of microwaves) and then sows rows of wheat, oats, and sugar beets:

the seeds will be specially encapsulated, containing moistur-
izers to take account of any drought situation and moisture
inhibited should there be a downpour, weeds herbicided,
fertilized and bug protected. When the field is full of reapable
crops, along comes the computerized micro-factory machine
to reap all (the seed capsules incidentally will be time programmed so that the diversified crop matures all at the same
time, so that such a harvest is possible). The crops pass
through to the processing part of the machine where they
are crushed, mixed and baked, chocolate chips added and
then the cookies are processed, packaged, and palletized.

A future history map from the 1980s also brings human
cybernetic people amplifier appliances, knowledge-based
systems and robots. In the 1990s, from extrapolated technology trends, we can expect even smarter machines, and the
world linked robots and people amplifiers, while in the next
century, perhaps 'slaves' for robots!

Such technology advances are thus in the process of manipulating societies of the future.

Safe predictions for the next phase of semiconductor
integration developments include VLSI and VHSI passing
from tens of thousands of logic gates per chip into and
beyond the hundred thousand range — perhaps even by the
midpoint of the 1980s decade. The ever-present obstacle —
which always exists five to ten years before a future technological event becomes a reality — is the current question
of 'what to do with 100,000 gate chips'; this will surely be
solved early in the 1980s. One answer, to be hinted at later,
is the process of putting applications on a chip, such as MIS-
on-a-chip (Management Information System).

But, and here is the rub, three new conditions arise for
our rapidly changing field. First, the number of alternative
applications possibilities of what to do with 100K, and later
million gates chips is extremely large: computers-on-a-chip,

smart-machines-on-a-chip, applications-on-a-chip, programs-on-a-chip, signal-processing-on-a-chip, compilers-on-a-chip, data-management-on-a-chip . . . Secondly, the design-development investment for each is huge, both in time and cost. But if more than a million copies are made of each, millions of dollars of development costs, add only a few dollars to each copy. Finally, the number of components of 100K gate size, even in an elastic market, is quite a bit less (than previous chip components in the LSI and MSI ranges) for each design — but, more in total for all usefully possible 100K gate chip application designs. When these force factors for the future are combined, they suggest that VLSI, VHSI, and BHSI (beyond VHSI) should have much longer lives than MSI and LSI hardware — both for their use in systems, as well as for their design life viability as a primary component of future systems.

Another forecastable obstacle, and perhaps the biggest problem area, is the software problem — e.g., it is the stretch out in time imposed for the design of 100,000 gate chips — the Computer Aided Design (CAD) problem. That is, the pacing element is the catch-up game required by CAD developers, and program developments, to keep pace with rapid semiconductor technology developments. Here again, if VLSI or VHSI truly turns out to have a longer life, so should the resulting CAD and Operating System (OS) support systems.

With tens of thousands, hundreds of thousands, and millions of logic gates per component — as with even a few thousand per chip — there are long design times. Because of such long design times, the component hardware for new computer systems for initial use early in the 1980s is already in existence on designers' desks. Further, the design-development time for computers — large or small — is even longer, and a serial add-on to the design time for the basic hardware components. Computer systems for the early 1980s thus have already had their design cast on the prints. In fact, the time from the technology design inception of a new computer system to its first real usage/impact is well beyond five years, with common (or peak) usage not occurring until near the tenth year; by the twentieth year, it is still a usefully viable system — and this time scenario is expected to grow longer.

Thus, interestingly, even in the face of an increasing pace of technologically innovative developments in the underlying component technology, computer systems using such technology are tending to stay around longer as part of the technological fabric of society. This implies that (1) there is a considerable growth in the batching of computer function innovations and (2) there are a growing number of technologically backward (but not necessarily obsolete) computer systems in use, and that more are forecastable for the future. For some applications — especially in colleges and universities, research applications, the military — the hardware in use is inadequate relative to what technological advances would allow to be available. While for most others, perhaps the major number of applications, such computer systems using older (out-of-date?) technology are entirely adequate and desirable from the viewpoint of the system stability implied. But for the former applications, what is implied is a vast updating and revamping of computer systems for the mid-1980 decade or sooner. The successes from such computer developments will certainly impact all other areas of computing by creating more cost/performance-effective computer systems.

Thus, some time in the 1980 decade, we must forecast a turning point has already been initiated from the component viewpoint; it is the US government's VHSIC program turning point has already been initiated, from the component viewpoint; it is the US government's VHISIC program

scheduled for first impacts in the 1983 to 1985 timeframes —
with numerous computer developments expected to follow.
This computer hardware technology advance is adding analog
(signal processing, communication, and sensor) circuitry side
by side with digital logic and memory — resulting in an
entirely new type of hardware for designers to design next
generation computers.

Thus, even though we must forecast that the early 1980
decade computers will (only) be evolutionary enhancements
of present generation computers, we also must forecast,
for the latter part of the 1980 decade, revolutionary
computer developments — but perhaps not until almost the
1990s, unless non-technological factors cause a speed-up of
the introduction of such advanced technological developments.

As computers become more automatically cybernating
devices, in the form of appliances for amplifying people,
increasingly they will be called and characterized as 'ethnotronic' — a coined word pieced together from ethnic and
(elec)tronic roots. Why? Such purposive appliances (tools for
helping people) possessing communication capabilities,
meshed with computer/cybernetic smarts, will establish a
sort of ethnotronic culture — an electronic culture wherein
(1) people communicate with appliances, (2) appliances
trigger conversations with people to make the person they are
amplifying 'currently aware', and (3) appliances 'talking'
with other machines for the purpose of amplifying the person
served. Additionally, such amplifier appliances, in their own
'cultural ways', will supply/support many other human needs
by performing certain (broadly) information related, or knowledge and decision assistance based, tasks themselves in order
to perform their role within society.

Additionally, breakthroughs in mass storage technology,
in the coming decade, will see the creation of very large,

computer-stored data bases economically feasible for even small organizations — orders of magnitude larger in capacity, and at least an order of magnitude less costly. There is no doubt that one to two orders of magnitude drop in mass storage costs will have profound business and societal effects and impacts: quicker movements into the information society, higher economic productivity, massive jumps into the paperless future-office-of-the-future, real-time and life-long educational systems, knowledge (instead of data) based computer systems, and much more, including business and society infrastructure changes. Yet such advances in mass memory development are now clearly in store for the 1980 decade, and before 1990 we should expect even more.

FUTURE GENERATION 'CALCULATORS'

Instead of just developing more exotic ways of performing mathematics, envision a branch of calculator evolution turning toward amplifying individuals in their profession via people amplifier devices or appliances. That is, consider identifying a small number of primitive functions, for example, four, unique to management that can be cast in hardware which is programmable (button pushed and later via voice) and is like a microprocessor. Consider, also, another four primitives which are unique to auditing or accounting — another group unique for the medical profession, etc. — and that for each case a set of these primitives is built into the hardware of a hand-held device much like the modern calculator. Assume that they are instead called 'people amplifier appliances', a different one for each profession. Or, alternatively, besides a keyboard, the primitive functions, and some sort of a simple electronic display, that they also contain communications capability (e.g., can be plugged into, or go — wireless — to the telephone), considerable writable memory capacity (for holding information, the replay of and the query to a data base equivalent to a number of books or a file cabinet), and a sophisticated electronic display. For such sophisticated portable devices, we would no longer refer to them as a smart or intelligent terminal; rather, they most likely would be classified as information appliances. In either case, a multiplicity of appliances should hit the marketplace early in the 1980 decade, such as: smart management machines, smart doctor machines, smart reporter machines, smart voter machines, smart senator machines, smart programmer machines, smart designer machines, smart artist machines, smart teacher machines, smart student machines, and many others.

Each would become 'smarter' (evolve) through the addition of more primitives every three or so years. That is, many waves of evolutionary developments (generations of) of such smart appliances would be sprung upon the marketplace. Ultimately, the market for such people or information appliances totals many per person — billions of appliances.

As people appliances change toward information appliances, the need grows for larger and larger 'centralized' computers, or at the very least, very large and smart data bases. That is, the macros are needed to 'feed' such micro appliances with updated information. Thus, the more little ones (the information appliances) society uses, the more big ones (next generation more or less classical computers) are required.

FUTURE OFFICE-OF-THE-FUTURE

Much has been recently written about the 'electronic-office' and 'automated-office', or in other words the Office-of-the-

Future. Some such offices now exist and others are being planned. However, technology is rapidly advancing. As a result, many new options for the office-of-the-future are developing with many more expected on the future horizon for the 1980s. Thus, the office-scape of the future can now be forecast to go through a number of eras or generations as the future springs forth, somewhat mappable as shown in Figure 3.

In the mapping of the probable future history of the office-of-the-future, the later trends of MIS-on-a-chip/wafer, or the office-of-the-future-on-a-chip/wafer, brings about a 'component information system' or a 'component office' which is embeddable into other machines to make them smarter.

1 WORD PROCESSING (WP) — MINICOMPUTER BASED	6 COMPUTER MAIL AND COMPUTER CONFERENCING
2 SMART WORD PROCESSING — MICROCOMPUTER BASED	7 SMART OFFICE MACHINES — PEOPLE AMPLIFIER APPLIANCES
3 COMMUNICATIONS ORIENTED WP	8 SMART OFFICES
4 WP and DP (DATA PROCESSING) MARRIAGE	9 INFORMATION APPLIANCES
5 INTEGRATED WP-DP-MIS (MANAGEMENT INFORMATION SYSTEM)-DB (DATA BASE)-DBMS (DATA BASE MANAGEMENT SYSTEM)	10 KNOWLEDGE BASED MACHINES
	11 REMOTE OFFICES
	12 MIS-ON-A-CHIP/WAFER
	13 OFFICE-OF-THE-FUTURE-ON-A-CHIP/WAFER

Figure 3   Some Possible Future Office-of-the-Future Generations

In Figure 4, some mid-to-late 1980 and 1990 decade purposive ethnotronic people amplifier appliances and systems are noted. Obviously, each will start out as primitive embodiments and grow in capability thereafter as new versions enter the marketplace. That is, every few years after their initial introduction, wave after wave of advances should produce a series of follow-on generations. By the close of the 1990 decade these ethnotronic systems should become

ETHNOTRONIC SYSTEMS — SOLID STATE CULTURE	
1ST GENERATION	**2ND GENERATION**
SMART MACHINES	SMART SYSTEMS
BOOK-ON-A-CHIP	OFFICE-ON-A-WAFER
MIS-ON-A-CHIP	SCHOOL-ON-A-WAFER
COURSE-ON-A-CHIP	LIBRARY-ON-A-WAFER
DOCTOR-ON-A-CHIP	FACTORY-ON-A-WAFER
MANAGER-ON-A-CHIP	INSTITUTION-ON-A-WAFER
TEACHER-ON-A-CHIP	FUTURE WORLD(S)-ON-A-WAFER
POLITICIAN-ON-A-CHIP	CULTURES-ON-A-WAFER
PEOPLE AMPLIFIER APPLIANCES	

Figure 4   The Silicon Revolution: What Will Its Future Bring?

extremely capable and can then be forecasted drastically to
alter the infrastructure of society. Therefore, because we can
now forecast major changes in society to occur as a result of
developing future computer (type) systems, the responsibility,
on their developers and their future users, demands the early
study of such expected impacts and consequences — so that
society can get ready for such major impacts, in order to
change them into opportunities, rather than waiting to react
to them as a problem. The future worlds and cultures-on-a-
wafer can also be considered as new forms of 'dynamic
books' — for example, science fiction-on-a-wafer which
allows a dynamic (alterable) simulation of the fiction being
audibly and visually displayed (either in two or three dimensional form).

COMPUTER FUTURE HISTORIES

Thus, from these foregoing technological developments, the
pace of the computer's impact upon business and society is
expected to quicken in the 1980s.

Some new directions in microsystem technology resulting
in new cybernetic computer machine developments are:

Smart machines
— Smart computers
— Smart office, factory, educational, and transportation machines
People amplifier appliances
— Para-expert amplifier adjuncts
— Smart management, doctor, lawyer, auditor, teacher, etc., appliances
Component computers
— Computers-on-a-chip
Applications-on-a-chip/wafer
— MIS-on-a-chip
— Payroll-on-a-chip
— Order-processing-on-a-chip
Information appliances
— Smart-office-of-the-future-on-a-chip/wafer
— Remotable offices/schools
Smart memory
— Very low cost mass memory
— Smart data base memory/computer
Knowledge-based systems
— Libraries/file-cabinets-on-a-chip
Very large scale distributed computers (but physically small)
— DDP (Distributed Data Processing) (almost) everywhere.

A basic premise is: semiconductor silicon technology continues to advance sufficiently fast such that for the 1980s and beyond, computer developments will continue to emerge, which can be forecast to bring:

Less costly systems
More capable computer systems
More reliable, fault-tolerant, and self-repairable computer systems
Easier to use (friendlier) computers which are convivial

Physically smaller computers for embedding into things
to make them smart

More computer functionality

Amplification of people computers.

Further, these desirable impacts from future computer
technological developments can come at a faster pace for the
1980s than they have been emerging in the 1970 decade, that
leads to silicon based technology that is more widespread in
use and brings friendlier computers. This new technological
revolution is the era of convivial technology. It is the era of
embedding component-computers into things like computers, office-machines, factories and factory machines, auto-
mobiles, offices and office-machines, and the like, to make
such machines smarter and easier to use. In the 1980s, the
technological micro-engines of social change that allow smart
machines are the tiny silicon chips containing on their surface
tens, to hundreds of thousands, to millions of very fast
circuits in submicron geometries, and later the use of total
wafers for componentizing total applications, systems, and
much more. By embedding such micro-engines of extreme
logic complexities into common machines (and at their interface with humans) future technological systems can be forecasted into an era of an advanced 'convivial' symbiosis with
humans and the surrounding environment automatically
simple in application. All of this comes with continually
plummeting prices and with progressively increasing functionality and performance capabilities. Such declining prices
will allow micro-engines of change to become commonly
available, and with their convivial enhanceabilities (through
embedding of complexity to make the resulting systems easy
to use) allow the total world to benefit — rich or poor, expert
or non-expert, educated or educationally deprived.

Such visions of this desirable turning point in computer
technological developments, and the futures implied, make

it now possible realistically to extrapolate in the 1980 decade, from evolutionary extensions of the leading edge of today's technology. In peering through the maze of future technological trends and social forces at work, rapidly advancing evolutionary change, in retrospect, will look like radical revolutionary change when viewed over a ten-year or longer time span, especially as future computer developments allow computers to pass into new (lower) levels of affordability.

As previously stated, the current revolution in computers is measured in chips, microns, and nanoseconds, with the micro-engine of change being the tiny but highly integrated circuit silicon chip. Soon, silicon parameters are headed toward wafers, submicrons, and picoseconds as the technology pushes toward VHSI.

Although such parameters are important to semiconductor manufacturers and computer designs, what do they mean to the typical business person? The future impact of such hardware advances on computer systems, for the coming decade, can be forecast and summarized as follows:

More reliable systems
— Fault-tolerant and self-repairable
Easier to use systems
— Smart computers
Data base computers
— Smart memories
More processing options
— Application adjunct processors
More software cast in hardware
— Application primitives — programs cast into hardware
'Knowledge based' systems
— Integrated decision support systems
More distributed systems
— Smart DDP
— Smart machines

More computer networks
— Data communications
— Computer mail and computer conferencing
Next generation(s) office-of-the-future
— Greatly improved office productivity
— Smart offices.

SOFTWARE CAST INTO HARDWARE

Throughout the history of computers, as each new wave of
computers emerged, a growing number of (parts of) programs
were put into the hardware architecture — trends toward
'hard software'. In the pre-first generation, before the early
1950s, most computers did not have the sequenceable and
combinational primitive instructions wired-in, such as multiply and divide. And for many programmers, like myself in
my early career, much of their effort was spent in the programming of multiply and divide. Then, in the first generation of computers, these primitives were wired into the
hardware and thus released programmers from such tasks —
allowing them more time for the application programming
effort than for controlling and manipulating the 'tool'.

The historical map and the extrapolation of the trend of
putting programs into hardware unfolds as 'eras of hard
software', such as:

1st hard software generation — 1950s (Early)
— Instruction/Computational primitives — e.g., multiply
  and divide.
2nd hard software generation — 1960s
— Algorithmic primitives — e.g., indexing, floating point,
  trig functions, and square root.
3rd hard software generation — 1970s
— Language/Control primitives — e.g., executive control

primitives, I/O (Input/Output) primitives, HLL (High Level Language) primitives, microprocessor primitives, and system primitives.

4th hard software generation — 1980s
— Application primitives — e.g., peopleware primitives, profession (e.g., management) primitives, accounting primitives (e.g., payroll), etc., MIS, and courseware primitives.

1985 (After)
— General system primitives.

1990s
— Institutional primitives and robotic primitives.

In most cases, for the 1980s, the future primitives for hard software will: (1) be incorporated as part of the hardware architecture of computers or 'calculator' devices; (2) be cast as an optional adjunct for attachment to a computer system, memory, a calculator, or to an information appliance to make them smarter, or otherwise (3) become a stand-alone, special-purpose machine — for example, a 'payroll machine' or an 'electronic file cabinet'. Some time toward the mid-to-late-1980 decade, smart people/information appliances could well become the major interface to computers, data bases, information bases, and knowledge-based systems.

CONCLUDING REMARKS

Future computer technology is thus forecasted to cause an economy-of-scale flip-flop. That is, as computers and other machines become smarter, more computer power will become distributed in local machines and to aid individuals. Further, these same technology trends are forcing computers of all classes to be physically small and to be cast from micros. Thus, the micro era computers initiated in the 1970s will grow in the 1980 decade and the trend away from macrosystems to microsystems will continue. In this characterizing of the coming era, (1) components will become end products; (2) computers will become components; (3) ethnotronic people amplifier computer appliances will become common; and (4) schools, offices, factories can now be forecast to become machines (made from component computers) for the longer range future. For the latter, vast energy savings are possible; therefore, such a future largely depends upon the course that the energy crisis takes in the 1980s. After the 1980s, perhaps early in the 1990s, when multiple systems are integrated onto wafers, the 1990s could again be characterized as the macro era of computers (but not from the physical size viewpoint).

Does all this mean the demise of large centralized main frames? Most likely it does not. Trends are now indicating that the more computer power is remotely distributed, the more computer power is required at central nodes, to support both traditionally centralized functions and also to support the remoted/distributed systems and devices, such as the forecasted people amplifiers and the carried-information appliances. Thus, even in the 1980 decade, we can forecast a growth in macrosystems. In fact, we might label the very late 1980 decade the rebirth computer age of the macrosystems, as we are labelling the 1970s the microsystem era. That is, as hardware costs continue to drop and more computer functions are put on a chip or wafer, business, science, and society will have the opportunity to tackle much larger problems with computers.

Thus, many of the social aspects (taboos and forbidden zones) that currently exist are apt still to exist in the next decade (in respect to the use of 'older computer systems') together with many new ones (in respect to the emerging future ethnotronic systems).

Does this imply that DP people and management will have less to do, or even be phased out? Most certainly not — except for certain application areas. Why? First of all, for those applications that we learn to almost completely automate, and thus cast into hardware, DP personnel and management will largely not be required. But because computers can still be forecasted to become smaller, considerably less costly, more applicable, more functional, more capable, and more reliable, we must also forecast that they will: (1) be in more widespread usage; (2) therefore need more support services; and (3) create more applicability into both smaller and bigger application areas — all pointing toward the need for more DP personnel and management. But, needless to point out, future DP management will be increasingly displaced and the task will be considerably altered — even so, a bright future for DP management is forecastable, especially in an environment of cohabitation with friendly computers.

Further, future smart machines and ethnotronic systems will certainly change the infrastructure of the office, the factory, and later most of society. Thus, it is not too early to start their study and forecasted societal impact analysis in order to impact their design toward needed and desirable directions — and most importantly, in order to capitalize on the opportunities that their supervention makes possible. But also, to find the future taboos and forbidden zones to avoid by impacting our designs and usage, ahead of time, before they become problems for society to react against. Further, since future computers will free resources, people, energy, and capital as well, they provide the means for enterprises to move into new ways for providing (new) product and services for raising the societal quality-of-life — and to create new jobs, to fill the void created when jobs are displaced by smart machines. But we must study and research such futures in order that society knows, ahead of time, so that society can prepare for such new jobs and new futures. That is, our responsibility is increasingly to do the R&D, and to inform the public about the alternative desirable ways the future can be pushed (so that society can choose) in order to avoid or eliminate the negative social aspects.

In the final analysis, future computer developments, by the late 1980 decade and thereafter, are going to present many alternatives. Yet many, if not most, of the computers now in use will still be in use together with many follow-on (evolved) versions. Additionally, new computers, both larger and smaller (in capability) types, which are considerably smarter and more cost/effective, will also proliferate. But perhaps the most used computer type in the later 1980 decade will not even be called (or referred to as) a computer — it will be a type of 'component computer' embedded into other machines (including both old and new computers) to make them smart and easier to use. Thus 'computers' could become relegated to a new status — they could become the nuts and bolts of systems.

14 COMPUTING TECHNOLOGY AS SEEN FROM 2979 AD
Is the Electron Here to Stay?

Rex Malik

*Rex Malik has been called 'the doyen of European writers on elec-
tronics and computing.' He is currently a columnist of the journal*
Computerworld, *and has worked extensively in radio and television.
His books include* And Tomorrow . . . The World? Inside IBM *and*
The Viewdata Revolution *(with Sam Fedida).*

You will, I hope, forgive me if I begin with one of the most
hackneyed cliches of the last thousand years: 'Is the electron
here to stay?' It was a question which I can first trace as
being asked, albeit in a frivolous fashion, around the time
which forms our starting point, the year 1979. I would have
thought that a question which had been asked now for
around 1000 years and to which the answer has so far been:
'Yes, as far as we can foresee', would have ceased to be a
question to which one should pay much attention. However,
it seems that there are still people who do not find the
answer satisfactory. So, let me state it again.

As far as we can see, the electron remains the key to our
ability to compute (a term with which some of you may be
unfamiliar and which we shall deal with shortly). It is the
critical element in digital technology, has been so for over
1000 years, and, though other ways of handling information
have been suggested, in the end we are forced back to the
electron and electronics.

If this binds us to our predecessors of 1000 years ago, so be it. I shall try to concentrate, however, not so much on what binds us, but the differences between us. And, I shall try to discuss with you the reasons for some of the differences: this is the true territory of the technological historian.

It is a difficult exercise to do, particularly as I am going to eschew social history: I am going to have to separate from our culture techniques and artefacts which we would not consider to come within the realm of the technological historian, but, rather as coming within that of social decision.

And this is an immediate difference between us. You see, what we are going to have to do is to look at the technology of a set of civilisations and cultures which were taking their first, faltering steps on the road to technological dependence, cultures which had not yet come to terms with it. You will find this inconceivable today, but one thousand years ago, they were arguing whether or not those steps should be taken, not realising that the choice was no longer with them: they were already committed.

I intend to concentrate on the differences between the years 1979 and 2979, leaving out the intervening period. And I intend to concentrate mostly on hard technology and approaches to systems. The contrast between the times separated as they are by a thousand years, is well worth making even if it is a difficult one for us, who look back with the benefit of hindsight and sometimes wonder why it was that they did what they did. Hindsight, however, is what they did not have. We have to remember that what we see as their limitations, was seen by them as normality. They accepted it, indeed they were often excited by it, and they did the best they could.

Yet they were a remarkable people, for they discovered two fundamental precepts which have stood us in good stead, even if those precepts were understood by but a few. One, they realised, that in the case of the technology we are considering, there were few technological limits — at least for them: that the technology was capable of much further development. You must not laugh of course, looking back on their technology, it had to be capable of further development.

It followed, therefore, that computer power and its provision were not likely to be a serious problem for future generations: the technology could be invented. Now I realise that the phrase, computer power, will be unfamiliar to most of you present here today. We have, after all, grown up in an era when the notion of such a measure is inconceivable: for to talk in terms of computer power after all indicates that there must have been a shortage of supply, and it was so.

The second precept follows. It is much more fundamental and important, and, in this sense, they are our true ancestors. They are the first generation to realise that you could invent yourself out of a problem, that a long term crisis could be made to go away by consciously setting out to invent its solutions. That is one notion we owe to them, and let us not forget that they were the first to see it, and to begin to develop their societies accordingly.

These, however, were ideas whose time was coming. What was it like before their time did? Firstly, our remote predecessors' ingenuity far transcended their simple technology. Were this not meant to be a celebration of a thousand years, I should be tempted to go back thirty more years and show you how even more primitive were the systems with which their immediate predecessors coped. Their ingenuity? You have to remember that we are discussing the century in which powered flight, nuclear power, optical means of transmission, working at the molecular level, all began, and the period in which the first tentative steps into the solar system were taken. One is indeed surprised that given their technology, any of those were achievable at all.

You may well laugh again when I tell you that just ten years before the time we are considering, the majority of computers (I am sorry, but I am going to have to use this antique terminology: their systems were primarily used to work on and with numbers, and the term was, to them, normal and natural). The point I wish to make was this, their computers were so organised that if you wished to make a simple calculation, one requiring any aid of machines, you had first to assemble your data, put it on paper or tapes, take it with you to what they called a computer centre — I mean by that physically visit it — hand the data, and sometimes the programs — their concept of program, incidentally, was somewhat different from ours — over to the system's 'operators', who would then look at it and, more often than not, tell you to come back tomorrow, sometimes indeed as far off as next week, when you would be given the answers. And, even then, there was little surety that the answers would be those you were seeking, or were indeed correct.

This situation, of course, still exists in some rarefied areas, and we shall deal with those in a minute. But it is not a situation with which most of you will be familiar.

So, let us now try to break down the differences between our ancestors by considering the major differences, the major distance between us. The first and most critical was the formal separation of hardware and software, and, it is the second of these with which I wish to start. And I wish to tackle it in its broadest sense. What we mean by software is now very different from what they meant by software. To them, software was primarily programs, programs which were separate to machines and artefacts. Now the notion that the process of systems creation is a two-stage process, in that one, you build a device which is inert, and, two, you make it useful by loading into it an instruction repertoire which has been laboriously thought out by people: that these are two separate processes, this is a very strange notion. At least, and I must enter the caveat here, to us. But, you see, they did not have the tools to create systems in which the processes to be carried out were inbuilt, and laid down with the circuitry. Of course, in some archaic areas we still write software in the sense in which they understand it, but this is a minor part of the software scene. To them, software had primarily to do with computers, to use it is a much more abstract, much more fundamental process with much, much wider implications, and, I may say, that they practised little of it.

If I say to you, software, you wlll immediately think of ways of organising information, you will think of structures, you will think of the problems involved in subsuming into our schema new knowledge, particularly knowledge which has inconvenient characteristics: it does not have a natural fit. But then, we cannot always expect that nature will be a tidy process. A famous thinker from the twentieth century once remarked that: 'The Good Lord is subtle, but he is not malicious', even though sometimes we may feel that the situation is the reverse.

You will think, too, of the ways in which we have tamed technology to us, something they were just beginning to worry about. But, you see, though our ancestors were becoming much exercised about structure and hierarchy, though they were beginning to have a slight understanding of the diversity of people, and their ways of thinking, all this was still at a trivial level. Thus, for instance, the theory of types was understood by mathematicians: its practical consequences outside the field were generally not. The notion that like devices by function had to be carefully graded and placed at their right place within hierarchies, and that this had to be replicated throughout all systems if you were to have compatability both at the mechanical level and the more abstract level, this was hardly grasped. And, they paid the penalty for it in the inability of like systems to communicate with each other.

I have already started some of the differences between us: let me give you some other major problem ahead where we differ. And, again, I will use their terminology.

I will begin with the area of linguistics: and this may well be the greatest surprise you have. You are used to a planet-wide technology: our ancestors were not, and this had consequences.

Computing technology was dominated by a handful of countries, mostly working within one language, English. Where the technology was by others, a knowledge of that language was often a necessity if you were to work at any serious level, for the literature was largely written in the English language, was not generally kept within the systems in use, and translations were difficult to arrange. You are listening to me in the language you find most comfortable, a painless process both at your end and mine. In their day, to achieve that would have required the use of human translators, one to a language, and would have been a cumbersome, expensive process to set up, and could not be presumed to be handled automatically on demand.

For they did not have automatic translators. And the reason they did not you may care to think about. We are so used to systemic inter-dependency that we do tend to forget they were not, they were just beginning to go down this route. Planet-wide intercommunications systems were in their infancy, only one of two systems were in existence and those were primarily military. It is only in the 1990s that we can begin to truly say that it becomes possible to talk to any part of the planet from any other part, as and when you please. And, even then, please remember that a surprisingly small number of people had this facility available to them: the notion that seventy-five per cent of the planets' inhabitants were cut off one from another, may be hard to comprehend but it was so. To have access, you must have access to the equipment. Most of the planet did not.

I turn now to the purposes for which their computers were used: and this I find the most unbelievable of all differences and the one hardest to credit. Nine out of ten of their computing engines, their installations were dedicated to the recording of past events. I exclude from this description the trivial uses to which they had put digital technology in control systems, I talk of systems which had a reasonable — for the period — information capability.

Now I do not mean that the technology was in the grip of historians, far from it, that, if you will excuse my bias, would seem to me to have been more useful. No, the technology was used to record events of the recent past: the use of cash and resources. The main task of the technology was to apportion these records to those who had responsibility for them: Did you owe me? Did I owe you?, and then go on to the settlement process. A major and related use was to keep track of where things were, and this is just as strange: not because they wanted to know the physical location of these things, but to keep track of their value, and to know who had them, and when they needed replacing.

That this minor subset of our usage should have assumed the importance it has says a lot to us about the shortages which were present in their societies. It was a useful discipline, but one taken to absurd lengths. Though, I must say that sometimes I think it is a discipline to which we ought to pay a little more attention.

You will notice that I have used the term Installation. It will, by now, have become apparent to you that their computers were, for them, expensive systems and of limited application. Indeed, given the handicaps they were under one can at times only marvel that they were able to handle information or compute at all. The technical shortcomings, indeed, were so severe that they made extensive use of people to do things that should be done by machine.

Hence the term Installation, a machine resource supported sometimes by many people: the operators I have mentioned, the so-called software specialists writing programs and, people manually using keyboard devices, preparing the data to be entered into the computer. The intelligent solution, the capture of data from source by the system, this was in its infancy.

From what I have said so far, you will have spotted a key difference between us. It lies in the area of communications: the concept of the interlinking of like computer resource with like resource was known to them, but little practised in any serious way.

You may laugh at the notion that one computer cannot correspond with another. Incidentally, I am sorry that I have to go on using this archaic terminology, but I do so because it is expressive and conveys quite clearly ideas which otherwise would be alien to us. Nevertheless, the concept of interworking of resource according to function, all enmeshed in a hierarchy, a system which itself apportions the type of resource required to handle a specific problem, this was alien to them.

Where we have networks, they had stand-alone systems. Now, you all know about stand-alone systems, even if they differ from those of our ancestors. And you know who has them: they are confined to geniuses and children, the first because they are not subject to rule, the second because they cannot be trusted to abide by it. We cannot have children trying to upset the planet, tying up its resources by trying to obtain answers to insoluble paradoxes, and, as you know that is what they are likely to do, given the chance.

But, let me continue with this problem of installations. The technology of 1979 was such that a powerful computing resource was also often a physically large resource. We have to be careful of this term, powerful; it is powerful in their scale of thinking, not ours.

The point is that it was large in size, and a considerable consumer of energy in the form of electric power. Which led to problems of heat dissipation, which in turn meant that they were housed in special, air-conditioned buildings. (Though, to be fair to our ancestors, the late 1970s through the 1980s are the years of transition when these problems were beginning to be overcome.)

Now air-conditioning was a primitive form of environment control; one then not widely used. I would guess, I have not looked it up, but we can do so if you wish, that no more than one per cent of the buildings in Europe had such a form of environment control. What is strange is that they should use it to look after machines, not people.

But, there was a reason: I said just now that their systems were large consumers of electric power, and that the resultant heat had to be dissipated. Their dissipation techniques largely consisted of letting the heat go to waste. True, there were a few installations where the heat was in turn used to help the cooling process, being piped off and transformed. But, this was as far as it went.

That a process was possible in which the heat generated could itself be used to pull in cooler air, and thus help to maintain the right temperature stability in the system was known to them. What they did not have was the materials. Porous ceramics with fast reacting properties to temperature changes do not come into wide use until well after the period that interests us.

We have to remember that the temperatures they worked with were generally far higher than those with which we are familiar. Indeed, I doubt that any safety inspectorate would today pass as safe any computer system operating at those levels.

I have to point out too, that the power levels were required for two reasons. One, the electronics were great power consumers. Two, they were also extensive users of mechanical devices linked to their systems.

You will all immediately think of one case of a computing system which has a large power requirement if operated in the wrong environment: the systems built on the principles of the Josephson junction, which require that temperatures be brought down to very near absolute zero before they can work. But those on earth, as you know, are a rarity. Indeed, Josephson, who was alive at this time, might be surprised at the use we have made of his work.

Though our ancestors in 1979 were primitively involved in working in space, indeed, in 1979 they were celebrating the tenth anniversary of the first manned landing on our moon, they knew singularly little of the cold of deep space, nor of the uses to which we have been able to put it. They had almost no conception of systems which have never seen earth or felt its gravity. The space industries had not begun.

It is possible that even without Josephson's work, we might have discovered the fast switching ability of some materials at near zero temperatures, it is open to doubt, however, whether so much could have been done so early. So remember, our ability to work with materials in their natural environment is a major difference between us.

They were earth-bound, we are not.

I now want to turn one of the lasting substances of civilisation: silicon. This is highly appropriate, as one thousand years ago they were much exercised about the systems it enabled society to create, and the place of people in what to them was going to be a new scheme of things.

But, their use of silicon was limited by their primitive fabrication techniques. We should not expect any different. That silicon had uses in the fabrication of computing systems had, after all, been discovered in their lifetime. They were at the beginning of the technology we all now take for granted.

We are indebted to one of the writers from the period, for a story of a problem with which they were confronted, yet to which they could not find a solution. The problem concerns the speed of light and its influence on computing operations. Some of the early devices though obviously requiring quite complex and cumbersome, manufacturing techniques — well, what do you expect of a society which made such wasteful use of people — faced a serious problem. The speed of operation was limited by the speed of light.

The reasons were twofold. First, at the software level (our software, not theirs) they were essentially builders of serial systems: you see the fix you can get into when you do not apply the theory of types. This led to circuits of quite incredible complexity, when you considered the tasks they performed.

But, that is looking at their world from our standpoint. Secondly, we are considering a technology in its infancy: irrespective of the use to which they put the systems they also had a fabrication problem. They were building circuits which could have as many as a quarter of a million switching elements in two dimensions. Ten years after 1979, they were to be found building them with a million switching elements. And, yet they were still two dimensional. Which meant that in sometimes simple circuits, the signals had to travel an inordinate distance.

So here is the story. Around this time one of the world's first programmers, Captain Grace Hopper of the United States Navy used to give lectures for which she kept a short

piece of copper rod the length of a nanosecond. And she used
to hold it up to her students and say, simply, 'We must do
something about the speed of light'.

I know that this will seem strange to you, but, as I have
remarked before their fabrication techniques were limited.
Silicon was new to them: even when they began to use it,
the majority of circuits were still put together from components, separate, each according to function, attached together on boards, connected by wire, and then slotted into
their machines. You can imagine how expensive and cumbersome the simplest of functions became to carry out.

Yet, the solution was available to them: it is our solution,
and, is one of the oldest techniques in use in the world. It
was to go three dimensional. It was initially made possible by
tools which were also available to them, the use of lasers to
etch circuit paths and the fine mesh of channel housings into
which we can inject the circuits themselves. That technique
has enabled us to reduce sizes dramatically. Allied with our
better understanding of power requirements, our cooling
techniques, it has made some drastic size reductions possible. But, and this is the important bit, it has given us computational and information handling capabilities of which
they could but dream.

Of course, as you know, we still use planar techniques,
except that ours are much more refined. Where they might
have as few as a dozen layers of connectors and insulation,
our ability to work at the molecular level has allowed us to
build interconnected layers in their hundreds. Indeed, so far
we have not found a limit simply because no one has been
able to suggest a system which is beyond our manufacturing
capability. Of course, it may be that the techniques are
limited. However, as these sorts of systems are themselves,
as you know, designed by systems, no human has ever
bothered to ask. The systems produce what we require of

them for the class of tasks which we expect them to perform. And, with all these technologies, there are of course exceptions.

I speak of the needs of scientists, or rather, their needs as they perceive them. In some respects, we have not changed, scientists least of all. From the start those scientists with a specific requirement for high-speed computation, particularly those immersed in physics, weather, and cosmology have been complaining that they never had enough power for computation, or that if we should provide the power to tackle a specific problem, it was not fast enough. This is probably by now the longest running complaint in the solar system.

The current complaint comes, as you know, from that branch of science known as cosmological physics. The complaint there, as I expect you will all be aware, is that they cannot model the activity of our sun in what we call normal time, and what our ancestors called real time.

It is no use pointing out to them that they are now trying to push us way beyond all known physical limits: that the interlinkages required within the computational system they say they need, however they are made, themselves create a speed boundary.

They indicate that what they wish to do is to simulate, and to do that they think that even an elementary sun model requires that they have an intermix of computation and on-line storage of around 10^{16}: and this in normal time.

In case you have forgotten, or are feeling too lazy to call the data up, let me remind you of that most powerful of all computing engines, the brain. It has between 10^{12} and 10^{15} bits on-line, and, as you will remember, even with the best available techniques of chemical enhancement, we have never been able to make it operate with more than 10^8 on-line concurrently, on any problem.

We have been able to model neuronal activity now for well

over 900 years, but, even now, if we wish to operate in normal time, we are limited to around 10^7 bit neural connections. It is the old problem of complexity which defeats us.

Fortunately, we are in many ways more knowledgeable than our ancestors: it would indeed be surprising if we were not. If I were to be asked here to pick from the change that has occurred in the last thousand years, our major success, it would not be in hard technology, but in one area of software: specifically our attack on the problems of complexity, at least, this planet-bound complexity.

We have achieved this in large part by our use of records and statistical techniques. The aggregation of a time series which runs on some problems for over a thousand years has had its uses. It has, for one, taught us to state that we have X or Y options, does not, of itself, give us any idea of the probability of those options. I know that there are some of you who will say that 1000 years plus is not enough, and who wish the human race had begun realistic record keeping some thousands of years earlier, but, at least, we are better placed than our ancestors 1000 years ago. They were, after all, operating much of the time with records which had only begun in their century.

What is surprising is how little of this our ancestors understood. It is not just that their technology was primitive, it is also that their thinking was also often more primitive than their ingenuity would otherwise lead you to believe.

Let me give you two examples of problems which exercised them. At the beginning of the exploration of space, at a time when they were just beginning to make use of orbital satellites, they began to survey the earth from space. They had a problem of picture analysis and comparison, a problem which they were unable to handle in normal time. The requirement was to compare one picture with another: to seek differences. I will not bore you with the calculations which lead to the conclusion, but it was estimated that a two-picture comparison would require computational power of between 10^{13} and 10^{14}, give or take the power of ten either way, to do a complete comparison in normal time. Yet, of course, the trained brain-eye combination can handle this in anything from seconds to minutes, at least for simple comparisons — where their system could take a week.

They did not understand how the trick was worked, and we should, in some ways, be grateful to them for that. It may seem a strange thing to say, but, had their thinking been better, we might not have obtained the advances in hardware technology and power that we have, and we could still be feeling the effects today.

The second example comes from the ancient game of chess. That a system could or could not play chess to Grand Master level much exercised our remote ancestors, and they argued about it at length. The argument was concerned with the number of options that the system would have to study before it could play chess to acceptable levels.

The mistake they made was to equate all possible moves with the search for the optimum move at any one time. The argument ceased many centuries ago as we began to be able to create true knowledge-based systems, so you will probably be unfamiliar with the requirement. Had we had to follow the evaluation of all possible moves route, we should have required a system of 10^{120} capability, if we are to assume that answers must be found within the time constraints under which the game of chess operates. It would, in other words, have had to operate at speeds far beyond that of light, irrespective of the system's architecture.

Yet, what they failed to remember was that the chess Grand Master operated, as I remarked earlier, with a system on his shoulders of 10^{15}, and worked, often successfully, within the time frame required.

You will, of course, realise the mistakes they made, interesting mistakes. The first was to equate the architecture of their systems with the architecture of the brain. I leave aside the thought that we are here talking of dissimilar organisms. The mistake was to think that devices which were essentially serial could in any way be compared with a brain system in which redundancy is high, and where operations are carried out in multi-dimensions, serial, parallel and concurrently, and, in which all memory was physically located within the processors.

The second mistake was to think that there was any need to carry out searches to this level. You will remember that I said a little earlier that we had an advantage denied our predecessors. We had a thousand years or more of accurate record-keeping behind us.

It is with that that we have been able to build knowledge-based systems. Now, few of their systems were knowledge-based. The reason is not that they did not understand that a system which contained enough data about the world in which it operated was preferable to one which did not: they understood that very well. It was that they had not been able to achieve it at any more than a trivial level; elementary controllers of devices and the like.

But, perhaps more important, they lacked memory, instantly available memory. Now this is not a trivial difference between us, it is a major difference. They had to strain themselves to achieve 2×10^6 in words of contiguous memory, which gave them immense problems. Complex arrangements had to be made to bring data down into working areas, data kept outside memory in storage devices.

And that in turn led to just as complex software arrangements — both in their sense and ours — having to be made to move this data around.

They had what they called operating systems, instructions

routines of sometimes inordinate size and length, to keep track of where everything was, move it around and actually carry out operations once the data was in an area on which it could actually be worked. Hence, you must not leave here with the idea that the two million words you could actually use were doing anything useful. Those operating systems had to reside within the processing area, which in turn could mean that it was reduced by a third.

And yet, to use one of their phrases, I kid you not, that operating software was usually machine dependent. Now, I did not say type of operation dependent, but, machine dependent. Their machines were built by a large number of organisations, each of whom made their own version. So you could not, even within functional classes of their systems, make two machines each from differing manufacturers run using the same operating software.

But I digress. I was saying that their systems lacked a knowledge base. We have here, at the dawn of the era of electronic systems, a very peculiar and interesting situation. The technical shortcomings meant that the few records they kept were not at all well used. Trend analysis, based on past historical data, which we take as the norm, was in its infancy. You may well say that as their records were so few, one should not expect much different. But nevertheless, some records they did have, certainly enough to carry out short term, say ten to fifty years, analysis. Yet they were in a poor position to use what they knew, if one considers that the existence of a record is equivalent to knowing about it as we do.

I would not like you to go away from here thinking that our ancestors were not clever, that the gaps in their thinking are inconceivable. We are, in fact, discussing one of the race's better periods. Indeed, there are some who would say that the intellectual flowering of the late twentieth century is unique in the history of the race. Those who take this line, and I have great sympathy with them, argue that never before, or since, have people produced so much with so few resources available to them.

We can look back at a list of honoured names: Einstein, Ashby, Plank, Heisenberg, Wiener, Beer, Shannon, Forrester, Josephson, Baran, as well as the early pioneers who took us to the edge of space and marvel that, given the technological constraints they were under, so much was at all achievable. I talked about memory just now: can you conceive of a memory system which lay outside the processing parts of the system, itself dependent upon physical movement: that if you wanted to access data you had to physically move the media in which it was contained to a point where it became accessible. Yet, it was under these sorts of constraints that they had to work.

I have purposefully left out of the list of men whose work was worth celebrating two names: Norman Huber and Lawrence Pinneo, and those students in the field who were becoming restless and know the references can now relax.

Huber is obvious. It is after all a thousand years to the year since Huber obtained his key patent for electro-molecular propulsion. Indeed, in some ways this lecture could be considered a tribute to him.

What Huber discovered, and it sounds simple now, is that charge transfer theory had practical applications. Now, that an electron is in a fixed position, which can be known, but it is there for only the minutest portion of time, was known to our ancestors.

They knew too that even at this level, the basic laws of the universe applied: an electron cannot be in two places at once and, therefore, there must be a time interval before the electron that has moved from one position is replaced by another: that statement would not baffle a two-year-old.

He would not find it so obvious the idea that atoms and molecules can during this movement, for a measurable period of time, share electrons.

We are then dealing with movements which can be interrupted, delayed and otherwise tampered with. To tamper with them requires the creation of barriers to movement. What we do is to use a standard technique, known to our ancestors: we add measured traces of conducting elements to the pure elements in which the movement is taking place: we interrupt the electron transfer, delay its passage sufficiently to build a charge, and then influence it by the use of an electric current.

Our ancestors had great problems with the Huber effect, and for a long time the basis of the technology was beyond them. Time, said one of their writers, must have a stop. It was a mistake they made to think that it was around these effects that time did stop. They were confusing their inability to measure with the fact that the event itself was measurable, and thus recordable. We cannot blame them, they did not have the instrumentation.

Now, what is it that we know that they did not? Where our distant forefathers made their mistake was to think that the movement of electrons, whether or not induced by Huber's techniques, was a random phenomenon. What they really meant was that the tools they were using were of such a crudity that they were not up to the task imposed upon them. They were confusing observation with reality, and, that mistake has been made long before them, and is still made today. The experience, the history of studies of the solar system has been replete with similar examples for the last 5000 years.

But, we know that electron movements obey the standard laws of physics: they have regularity. The problem is to detect it. Which, of course, takes me back to statistics.

What Huber had come across, one thousand years ago, was a basic phenomenon. It was only after the EMP effect had been much studied that it became apparent that there was a connection between the movement of the electrons and their position at any instant, and the composition of the elements in the material in which the electron movement was occurring.

Much of what we now know we have had to learn the hard way, using statistical techniques, the recording of literally millions of experiments sufficient for us to create tables of movements and time delays, according to material.

I have reduced what would normally be a lecture in itself to a couple of minutes. I will take even less to remind you of what we have done with Huber's technology.

Initially, it was thought that the main use of EMP would be in switching. It was a long time before it was seen that, if we could chemically code data, we could create a memory technology which had an inbuilt sorting mechanism to enable us to find, and find quickly, data of the same type, a technology in which chemical coding would also be used for security. EMP has enabled us to create an archival technology far different to that which our predecessors knew.

It has had also one interesting effect. The use of Huber's technology has enbled us to build memory systems of a denseness unknown to our ancestors, with a consequent impact on retrieval and processing speeds. We may not have been able to answer Grace Hopper's question, what are we going to do about the speed of light? we have, however, made that less of a constraint, less of a problem.

Our ancestors would find, however, that they could easily recognise one area of our technology: that is output technology. They too used paper, screens and voice — though voice output was in its infancy, with limited vocabularies. They would, I think, have been surprised at our ability to specify to a system a material requirement, and have the system's answer by producing the artefact without any intervening human intervention in design and redesign: our ability to make the system itself do the checking.

They would have been surprised also by our graphics capability: our ability to create three dimensional moving pictures which come from the imagination, yet look real. And yet there is no secret to this which they would not have been able to understand. They too had an elementary three dimensional graphics capability. What they did not have was enough digitally stored real picture data to act as a library which the system could use as an on-line reference point so that if you drew say a purple sky above Ulan Bator, the system could make the point that those can only exist in imagination. Did you wish a real sky, or the one you imagined?

They might not have thought of it as such, but that too is an output technology.

They were much exercised in the 1970s and onwards by what they called man machine symbiosis, would the man machine combination produce something which was better than either could do separately? This is an archaic question, one that has not been asked for some hundreds of years and which you will find strange for it is doubtful if any of us here today could conceive of a civilisation in which that question needed to be seriously put.

For that is the way *we* work. I have not touched so far on that other technology which we all rely on which also had its birth in the period we are considering. I refer to the technology which comes from the work of Dr Lawrence Pinneo, whose best work was done in the 1970s. Many of you will have used the technology based on Pinneo's work before you came here today, even if you have no idea who its initial creator was.

I refer to the technology of thought to thought communications and processing. For it was Pinneo who first put to use those unique properties of the brain rhythms to create a system. Pinneo did not discover that the EEG trace for each word and thought is unique to the individual, he did, however, invent the technique whereby we can store these in systems, and recall at will by thinking them. And thus of course having recalled the trace, it is but a simple process to convert it to convey words and messages.

It is that technique which has become the mechanism for civilised communication among adults separated by distance. It is that technique which has enabled us to do away with much of the message handling systems which consumed so much of the resources of this planet.

It is that technique which too has allowed us privacy, allows us to lock away our thought records and personal diaries.

This lecture has done little more than hit the highlights of the difference between the technology we use and that used by our ancestors.

I have not talked today of some major areas where we use our resources differently from the ways in which they were used by our ancestors. I have left out the whole area of robotics and their consequences. I do not think that our ancestors would have found the uses to which we have put the technology in those areas at all strange. Except, perhaps, that they might have been surprised by how anthropomorphism is a dead issue.

When we look back at their literature, we find it much exercised with the creation of robotic systems which look like man. But man is not a very efficient system for the majority of the tasks that need to be done: he is the best of generalised systems, yet in almost all special functions it is possible to design systems which are near optimal and turn out to look very little like him.

I have left out of this lecture too another system which much exercised them: this is the supersystem, an identifiable specifically located source of answers to all questions. And of course I have also left out the consequent fear that were such a system to be created, it would at some point decide that man in his own interests needed looking after whether he wished to be looked after or not.

We know of course that such a system is incapable of creation; that knowledge continues to expand at a rate which sometimes feels as if it is exponential without end. More importantly, we know that for the majority of questions we need to ask, this is the wrong way to go about it. Our data is spread around the planet and our communications makes possible access without our having to know where it is stored. We have not built a supersystem in the image of man, what we have are systems which are subject specific, and the tools between them to enable us to relate what needs to be related.

What I have tried to show you today is how much of our technology would have been recognisable to our ancestors. I would like to be around a thousand years from now to see whether our successors will find as few problems with us as I have found with our predecessors. Somehow, I do not think they will be too surprised.